I0448053

Four
Seasons, Four Moods
Spring Fatigue, Summer Lull, Autumn Depression, and Winter Blues

By
Alexandra Winter

Copyright 2024 Lars Meiertoberens. All rights reserved.

No part of this book may be reproduced in any form or by any electronic or mechanical means, including information storage and retrieval systems, without permission in writing from the author. The only exception is a reviewer who may quote brief excerpts in a review.

Although the author and publisher have made every effort to ensure that the information in this book was correct at the time of going to press, the author and publisher accept no liability to any party for any loss, damage or disruption caused by errors or omissions, whether such errors or omissions are due to negligence. accident or any other cause.

This publication is intended to provide accurate and reliable information with respect to the subject matter covered. It is sold on the understanding that the publisher does not provide professional services. If legal advice or other expert assistance is required, the services of a competent professional should be sought.

The fact that an organization or website is mentioned in this work as a citation and/or potential source of further information does not imply that the author or publisher endorses the information the organization or website provides or the recommendations it makes.

Please keep in mind that websites listed in this work may have changed or disappeared between the time this work was written and the time it was read.

Four
Seasons, Four Moods
Spring Fatigue, Summer Lull, Autumn Depression, and Winter Blues

Table of Contents

Introduction

Have you ever felt an inexplicable sense of excitement as spring blossoms unfurl, or found yourself sinking into a deep contemplative mood in the depths of winter? You're not alone. Our moods and mental well-being are remarkably intertwined with the ever-changing cycle of seasons. This book is here to unlock the secrets of these seasonal fluctuations and equip you with practical tools to navigate them effectively.

The changing seasons are more than just shifts in weather; they reflect a deeper, almost primordial rhythm that affects our inner worlds. Each season has a unique influence on our emotions, energy levels, and overall mental state. By understanding these seasonal effects, we can transform what might otherwise feel like insurmountable challenges into opportunities for growth and well-being.

In this pursuit, we will delve into how cycles of nature mirror the cycles in our lives, whether it's the rebirth of spring, the vibrancy of summer, the mellow tones of autumn, or the austere beauty of winter. We aim to make these natural rhythms work for you rather than against you, creating a harmonious existence that aligns with the world outside.

Our journey begins with recognising that some people experience significant mood variations with changing seasons, a phenomenon known as Seasonal Affective Disorder (SAD). SAD manifests as severe depression during certain times of the year, most commonly in winter.

Yet, it's not just limited to the winter blues; many experience subtler mood shifts as they cycle through the seasons.

Even minor seasonal mood changes can impact daily life. Feeling unusually tired in spring, sluggish during summer, or perhaps melancholic in autumn? These aren't mere coincidences; seasonal variations can gently nudge our mental state in different directions. Acknowledging these shifts is the first step towards mastering them.

The core idea of this book is balance. How do we maintain our equilibrium as the world around us transforms? We'll explore actionable strategies that encompass diet, exercise, mindfulness, and social connectedness—all tailored to the specific challenges and opportunities each season presents.

Spring, often seen as a season of rebirth and renewal, can paradoxically bring about both invigorating energy and perplexing fatigue. We'll unpack this paradox and offer ways to channel spring's revitalising force while mitigating its draining aspects.

Summer, with its extended daylight and warmth, provides ample opportunities for outdoor activities and heightened motivation. But for some, it also brings a lull—an overwhelming heat-induced inertia. Our strategies will help you harness the brightness of summer while staying cool and engaged.

As autumn rolls around, it brings a time of harvest and preparation for the colder months. Yet, it can also be a period marked by an onset of depressive symptoms for many. Here, we'll delve into understanding the trigger factors and ways to create comfort and connection that combat these autumnal blues.

Winter's stark beauty often comes with a predilection for introspection and reflection, but it also carries the risk of severe depression for those prone to SAD. Solutions like light therapy, maintaining warmth, and seeking social support can turn winter into a time of quiet restoration rather than overwhelming sadness.

Beyond individual seasons, it's vital to consider overarching lifestyle strategies that span the entire year. Diet plays a crucial role in mood management, and our exploration will include foods that boost your mood in alignment with each season's unique demands. Exercise is another powerful tool, and we'll help you find the right activity that fits seamlessly into the changing context of the seasons.

Good sleep is essential for mental health, yet our sleep patterns often clash with the seasonal shifts. We'll discuss aligning your sleep habits with these changes to ensure you're well-rested all year round. Likewise, mindfulness practices, such as meditation and breathing techniques, will be highlighted for their power to restore mental balance.

Engaging with the natural world and fostering community connections provide additional layers of support. Activities like nature walks and gardening can reconnect you with the earth, grounding your spirit. Building a supportive community through social activities or volunteering offers invaluable mental health benefits as well.

For those dealing with persistent seasonal mood disorders, understanding when to seek professional help is crucial. We'll cover special considerations for children, who also experience seasonal mood variations but may not articulate it as adults do. Addressing the workplace environment and its influence on our seasonal moods will also be a part of this comprehensive guide.

In essence, this book is a roadmap to thriving throughout the year. By aligning ourselves with the rhythms of nature, we can transform potential challenges into enriching opportunities. Let's embark on this journey together towards a more balanced, harmonious existence, attuned to the natural world's ebb and flow.

Chapter 1:
The Cycles of Nature and Our Lives

The rhythm of the seasons doesn't just dictate the colours of the trees or the temperature of the air; it also orchestrates subtle yet profound changes in our mental and emotional landscapes. Just as spring brings a burst of vitality and winter a time of hibernation, our moods and mental health are inextricably linked to these natural cycles. Understanding why we feel more buoyant in the summer and more reflective during autumn can unlock a wealth of strategies for harnessing these shifts to improve our well-being. Far from being passive observers, we can engage actively with each season's unique energy to create a life rhythm that promotes balance and growth. With foresight and a set of tailored approaches, we can transform seasonal challenges into powerful opportunities for personal development and emotional resilience, leading us towards a more harmonious and thriving existence year-round.

Understanding Seasonal Mood Variations

As the seasons shift, so too can our moods. Understanding these variations is crucial for navigating the ebb and flow of our mental well-being throughout the year. For many, the brightness of summer brings a lift in spirits, while the shorter, darker days of winter can lead to feelings of heaviness and introspection. These changes aren't just in your head; they're influenced by a complex interplay of biological rhythms, hormone levels, and environmental factors. Recognising how each season impacts you individually enables you to tailor your self-care strategies accordingly. By tuning into the natural cycles, you can pre-emptively address potential challenges, transforming them into opportunities for growth and self-discovery. So let's embark on this journey of understanding, to empower ourselves with the knowledge to thrive no matter what the weather brings. Remember, each season has its unique wisdom to offer, and with the right mindset, you can harness it to enhance your well-being all year round.

Seasonal Affective Disorder (SAD) manifests itself as a recurring issue for many individuals, marked by depression and lethargy during the shorter days of autumn and winter. Understanding SAD begins with acknowledging its real impact on mental health, which goes beyond mere 'winter blues' to a debilitating condition for some. Research suggests that SAD is linked to a biochemical imbalance in the brain prompted by the shorter daylight hours and lack of sunlight. In particular, a part of the brain called the hypothalamus may not work properly, affecting the production of melatonin and serotonin, which are crucial for regulating mood and sleep patterns.

When discussing Seasonal Affective Disorder, it's essential to consider the symptoms that set it apart from general mood fluctuations. These symptoms include persistent low mood, loss of interest in normal activities, irritability, feelings of despair, and in severe cases, suicidal thoughts. Additionally, many individuals experience changes in their sleep patterns, often wanting to sleep more but finding themselves less refreshed. Appetite changes, particularly a craving for carbohydrates and subsequent weight gain, are also common among those suffering from SAD.

One of the most compelling reasons to address SAD head-on is its potential to significantly disrupt daily life. Simple tasks may become overwhelming, and the overall quality of life can take a hit. Recognising these symptoms early and taking proactive steps can make a considerable difference. If you identify with any of these symptoms, it's vital to take them seriously, rather than dismissing them as mere seasonal discontent.

In tackling SAD, exposure to natural light is immensely beneficial. Light therapy, also known as phototherapy, has become a widely recommended treatment. It involves sitting by a specially designed light box that mimics natural sunlight. Typically, sessions last about 20-30 minutes a day, preferably in the morning, as this can help regulate sleep patterns and improve mood. However, it's crucial to consult with a healthcare professional before starting light therapy to determine the right type and duration of exposure.

Beyond light therapy, another effective approach involves supplementing your diet with Vitamin D. The body's natural production of Vitamin D is influenced by sunlight, and shorter days can lead to a deficiency. Including Vitamin D-rich foods like oily fish, fortified milk, and cereals in your diet—or taking a supplement after consulting with your doctor—can counteract the deficiency and support overall mental health.

Exercise also plays a pivotal role in managing SAD. Physical activity stimulates the production of endorphins, the body's natural mood lifters. Even when it's cold outside, trying to maintain a regular exercise regimen can help. Activities like brisk walking, jogging, or even indoor exercises can release tension, boost your mood, and help regulate sleep patterns. Combining physical activity with outdoor exposure, when possible, can provide the dual benefits of exercise and natural light, amplifying the positive effects.

In addition to these methods, cognitive behavioural therapy (CBT) has shown promise in effectively dealing with SAD. CBT works by addressing negative thought patterns and behaviours contributing to depressive states. Through guided sessions with a therapist, you can develop coping strategies that empower you to manage symptoms more effectively. With the right professional guidance, CBT can offer tools that extend beyond the seasonal episodes, providing long-term benefits for mental well-being.

The support of social networks can't be overstated. Isolation can intensify feelings of depression, making it critical to stay connected with friends and family. Even when you don't feel like socialising, maintaining at least some regular contact can provide emotional support and a better perspective. Simple gestures like a phone call or a coffee date can lift your spirits and foster a sense of community and belonging.

Creating a comforting and uplifting environment at home can also help mitigate the effects of SAD. Brightening up living spaces with warm lights, engaging in hobbies that make you happy, and even rearranging furniture to make the most of natural light can create a more inviting atmosphere. These small changes can make a daily difference in mood and outlook.

Mindfulness and relaxation techniques, such as meditation and deep breathing exercises, are powerful tools for staying grounded. These practices help you stay present, manage stress, and keep negative thoughts at bay. Integrating a few minutes of mindfulness into your daily routine can have profound effects on mental balance and resilience.

Another factor to consider is sleep hygiene. The disruption in sleep patterns often brought on by SAD necessitates a diligent approach to sleep hygiene. This includes maintaining a regular sleep schedule, creating a restful environment, and avoiding caffeine and screens before bedtime. Prioritising quality sleep can significantly affect mood and overall mental health.

It's also worth mentioning the role of nutrition in combating SAD. While the craving for carbohydrates might tempt you towards comfort foods, focusing on a balanced diet rich in fruits, vegetables, whole grains, and lean proteins can provide the nutrients necessary for sustaining energy and overall health. Omega-3 fatty acids, in particular, have been shown to support brain health and mood regulation.

If your symptoms are severe and persist despite these interventions, seeking professional help is crucial. Medication, such as anti-depressants, may be necessary and can be prescribed by a healthcare provider. Combined with therapy and lifestyle changes, medication can offer relief and help you manage SAD more effectively.

The importance of understanding and addressing SAD can't be emphasised enough. By employing a multifaceted approach that includes light therapy, diet, exercise, social connections, and professional support, you can significantly mitigate its impact. Rather than allowing the change in seasons to control your mood, taking these proactive steps can empower you to reclaim your mental well-being.

Remember, you're not alone in experiencing SAD. Many people face this challenge, and through shared experiences, support, and strategic interventions, it's possible to not just endure the darker months but to find ways to thrive through them. Implementing these strategies, being patient with yourself, and staying open to seeking help when needed are all essential aspects of managing Seasonal Affective Disorder successfully.

Minor Seasonal Mood Changes often go unnoticed, yet they play a significant role in our overall well-being. While not as intense as Seasonal Affective Disorder (SAD), these fluctuations in mood can still impact our daily lives. Understanding and recognising these subtle shifts is essential for maintaining mental health and turning potential challenges into opportunities for growth.

We don't always realise how profoundly the changing seasons affect our mood. Even minor variations in daylight, temperature, and weather can contribute to these subtle emotional shifts. For instance, as winter transitions into spring, some people may feel an inadvertent sense of renewal and vitality, while others may struggle with residual winter lethargy. Being aware of these tendencies can help us prepare and manage them effectively.

One aspect of minor seasonal mood changes is the increase or decrease in daylight hours. During the winter months, shorter days and longer nights can sometimes lead to a feeling of inner darkness. Conversely, when daylight extends in the spring and summer, we may experience a boost in energy and mood. It's not unusual to feel more optimistic and enthusiastic as the days get longer, but managing this surge of energy is just as crucial as combating the winter blues.

Temperature changes also play a part. The warmth of summer can be invigorating for many, encouraging outdoor activities and social engagement. However, extremely hot weather may cause fatigue and irritability. Similarly, the cool and crisp air of autumn can bring about a sense of freshness but may also trigger a pre-winter anxiety in some. By paying attention to how temperature shifts influence our mood, we can adjust our routines and self-care practices accordingly.

It's essential to differentiate between minor seasonal mood changes and more severe conditions like SAD. While minor fluctuations are common and manageable, SAD is a more intense and chronic form of seasonal mood disorder that may require professional attention. If you find that your seasonal mood shifts significantly impact your daily life, considering a consultation with a healthcare provider is a prudent step.

To navigate minor seasonal mood changes effectively, it helps to establish a routine that aligns with the natural rhythms of each season. For example, incorporating more physical activities and outdoor time during the sunnier months can improve mood and energy levels. Conversely, during the colder and shorter days of winter, focusing on indoor hobbies and relaxation techniques can help maintain mental balance.

One practical strategy is to adjust your diet according to the season. Fresh, vibrant foods in spring and summer can boost mood and energy levels, while hearty, comforting meals in the autumn and winter provide warmth and sustenance. Paying attention to your body's nutritional needs as they change with the seasons can make a noticeable difference in how you feel.

Exercise is another powerful tool for managing minor seasonal mood changes. Finding the right type of activity for each season can enhance your overall well-being. For instance, outdoor activities like hiking or cycling may be more enjoyable during the warmer months, while indoor exercises such as yoga or strength training can be more suitable for the colder seasons. The key is to stay active in a way that aligns with both the season and your personal preferences.

Sleep patterns are also influenced by the changing seasons. Longer daylight hours in the summer can disrupt sleep for some, while the extended darkness in winter can lead to oversleeping or feeling sluggish. Maintaining a consistent sleep schedule and creating a restful sleep environment can help mitigate these impacts. Simple practices like using blackout curtains in the summer and maintaining a regular bedtime routine in the winter can go a long way.

Cultivating mindfulness and relaxation techniques tailored to each season can be incredibly beneficial. Whether it's meditation, deep breathing exercises, or simply spending quiet time in nature, these practices can help ground you and provide a sense of peace throughout the year. For instance, practising mindfulness outdoors in spring can harness the renewing energy of the season, while indoor meditation in winter can create a cosy, reflective space.

Connecting with others is vital in managing minor seasonal mood changes. Building a supportive community and engaging in social activities can provide a sense of belonging and emotional uplift. Seasonal changes can sometimes bring about feelings of isolation, so staying connected with friends and family, whether through in-person gatherings or virtual meetups, can be immensely helpful.

Volunteering and helping others is another way to combat minor seasonal mood dips. Engaging in community activities or supporting a cause you're passionate about can provide a sense of purpose and fulfilment. Acts of kindness and giving back can enhance your mood and create a positive loop of emotional well-being.

Recognising and addressing minor seasonal mood changes is not just about avoiding the lows; it's also about embracing the highs and using them to your advantage. Each season brings unique opportunities for personal growth and connection. By being proactive and mindful, you can turn these subtle mood shifts into catalysts for a more balanced and enriching life.

In conclusion, minor seasonal mood changes are a natural part of the human experience. While they may not be as disruptive as more severe mood disorders, they still require attention and care. By understanding their causes and implementing practical strategies, you can navigate these seasonal fluctuations with grace and resilience, enhancing your well-being throughout the year.

Chapter 2:
Spring: Awakening and Fatigue

Spring is a peculiar blend of contradictions that often leaves us feeling both rejuvenated and weary. As nature awakens from its winter slumber, we experience a surge of energy akin to the blossoming flowers and longer daylight hours. However, this newfound vitality can paradoxically give way to a phenomenon known as 'spring fatigue'. The very season that promises renewal can also bring about a perplexing sense of exhaustion. The increase in brightness and activity might initially invigorate, but it also demands an adjustment from our bodies and minds that can be surprisingly taxing. Understanding this duality is key to navigating the challenges and opportunities that spring presents. As we delve deeper into the paradox of spring, it's crucial to balance our enthusiasm with self-care strategies that harness the season's potential while mitigating its fatigue. This chapter explores how to strike that balance, turning spring's enigmatic energy into a source of growth and well-being, setting the stage for the seasons to come.

The Paradox of Spring

Spring often comes with a burst of life and energy, yet paradoxically, many people experience bouts of fatigue and mood swings during this time. You might notice that while the world is waking up from winter's slumber with budding flowers and longer days, your body and mind are fighting a different battle. This juxtaposition of renewed vibrancy in nature against personal weariness can be bewildering. On one hand, there's an inherent excitement about the warmer weather and increased daylight, inspiring plans and activities. On the other hand, there is a physiological adjustment happening, which can leave you feeling unusually tired or emotionally drained. This is the paradox of spring: the simultaneous renewal and exhaustion. Understanding this duality is crucial in order to appreciate and align with the natural rhythms, ultimately leveraging the season's energy while managing its challenges. Balancing these conflicting experiences requires awareness and mindful strategies, which we'll delve into in the sections to come.

Renewed Energy vs. Spring Fatigue is a concept that's as captivating as it is perplexing. Just as the glassy frost of winter melts to make way for the vibrant promise of spring, many of us find ourselves perched on the edge of potential. The trees don their lush green garments, flowers unapologetically bloom, and the sun lingers a bit longer each day. This reawakening of nature often propels a buoyant sense of energy for many. But, there's a paradox at play here. Not everyone eagerly bounces out of winter's shadow. For some, the transition to spring can induce an unexpected weight—spring fatigue.

Consider this: As nature jolts back to life, so does your body's internal clock. The increased daylight and warmer temperatures compel your biological rhythms to adjust, sometimes dramatically so. For many, this surge in energy can be both invigorating and dizzying. It's almost like a shot of caffeine hitting an otherwise depleted system. You feel more alive, senses more acute, and even your mood may lift. But energy isn't uniform, and for some, the transition is tumultuous, leaving them grappling with a profound fatigue that almost seems incongruent with the season's vitality.

What's happening inside your body during this seasonal shift is fundamental. As your exposure to sunlight increases, your body ramps up its production of serotonin—a neurotransmitter often dubbed the "feel-good" hormone. Simultaneously, melatonin production, which helps regulate your sleep-wake cycle, decreases. Ideally, this should create a harmonious balance that fuels your days and rejuvenates your nights. But if this equilibrium is disrupted, you may find yourself feeling inexplicably tired even as the world outside becomes more energetic.

Could it be that your body is simply taking time to recalibrate? Quite possibly. Remember, nature doesn't rush, and neither should you. As the days grow longer, consider ways to ease into this new rhythm, rather than forcing yourself to match the world's accelerated pace. Gradual changes in your daily routine can help your body adapt more smoothly to the seasonal shifts.

But spring fatigue isn't just about biology. Emotional responses to seasonal changes are deeply personal and varied. Some people might feel overwhelmed by the busy schedules and social expectations that often accompany springtime's awakening. Others might struggle with the contrast between their inner state and the external world, feeling out of sync as nature moves forward and they don't.

Spring's paradox invites us to reflect: Is there more to this fatigue than meets the eye? Indeed, several lifestyle factors—ranging from diet to sleep patterns—can contribute to how we experience this transition period. Poor nutrition, particularly diets low in essential vitamins and minerals, can sap energy levels just as profoundly as a lack of sleep or excessive stress.

Interestingly, our ancestors may have been more attuned to this dichotomy, engaging in spring rituals and celebrations that acknowledged the need for balance. Think of traditional spring cleaning—not just of homes, but of mental spaces too. Refreshing your environment can mirror the internal purification, allowing you to shake off winter's lethargy in a measured, intentional way.

So how can you leverage this season's renewed energy while managing the fatigue that might come with it? Start by embracing natural rhythms. Pay attention to your body's cues. When the sun beckons, spend time outside to soak in its vitality, but balance it with restful moments designed to nurture your soul. Deploy a mix of gentle exercise and mindfulness practices to enhance your energy sustainably.

Nutrition plays a pivotal role as well. Spring often calls for a dietary shift—a movement away from the comfort foods of winter to lighter, more nutrient-dense options. Fresh vegetables, fruits, and lean proteins can provide the essential nutrients your body craves during this transitional phase. Keep hydrated by drinking plenty of water, and consider introducing herbal teas that offer both revitalising and calming properties.

Exercise can also be your ally. But here's the key: don't overdo it. Integrate a blend of cardiovascular activities and strength training exercises that can boost your serotonin levels without overwhelming your system. Walking, yoga, or even dancing can harmonise your energy levels, helping to combat fatigue while elevating your mood.

Another valuable strategy involves aligning your sleep with seasonal changes. While it might seem tempting to stay up later as daylight extends, maintaining a consistent sleep schedule can make a significant difference. Create a soothing bedtime routine, limit exposure to screens an hour before sleep, and ensure your sleeping environment is conducive to restful slumber.

Mindfulness can serve as both an energising and restorative practice. Techniques such as deep breathing, meditation, and journaling can help anchor you amid the seasonal flux. These practices allow you to tune into your thoughts and feelings, offering clarity and peace as you navigate the transition.

Don't underestimate the power of community connections during this time. Engage with family and friends, participate in group activities, or volunteer. Positive social interactions can bolster your mood and offset feelings of fatigue, reinforcing a sense of belonging and support.

The spring paradox—this dance between renewed energy and fatigue—invites a deeper understanding of ourselves and our connection with nature. Embrace it. Let it guide you toward a balanced approach to life's rhythms. Celebrate the resurgence of energy, but honour your moments of rest. In doing so, you will find a synergy that enriches not just your spring, but your entire yearly cycle.

The arrival of spring can indeed be an awakening, both exhilarating and exhausting. Acknowledge the duality and use the season as an opportunity for growth, continually learning and adapting. With mindful attention to your body, emotions, and environment, you can transform this paradox into a powerful period of personal renewal.

By embracing and managing both the highs and the lows of the season, you set the stage for a year of well-being and growth. Balance is the key—honour your energy, respect your fatigue, and thrive within the harmony of nature's rhythms.

Managing Spring Fatigue

Spring, with its vibrant blooms and promise of renewal, can paradoxically usher in a sense of fatigue for many. This phenomenon, often referred to as "spring fatigue," stems from the body's adjustment to longer daylight hours and fluctuating temperatures. To manage this seasonal lethargy, it's essential to synchronise with nature's own rhythms. Opt for a diet rich in fresh, seasonal produce and ensure regular physical activity to bolster energy levels. In addition, prioritise sufficient sleep and harness the benefits of natural sunlight. By making these mindful adjustments, you can transform spring fatigue into a period of revitalisation and growth, aligning with the season's inherent potential for renewal and well-being.

Embracing Natural Rhythms could well be the hidden key to managing the highs and lows that come with each passing season. Modern life often forces us into an unrelenting pace, disregarding the innate cycles of nature. But what if we consciously aligned ourselves with these natural rhythms? The benefits could be profound, ranging from improved mental health to enhanced overall wellbeing.

Understanding the patterns of nature allows us to make small yet significant adjustments in our lifestyle. Let's start with spring. As flowers begin to bloom, many of us experience a surge in energy. However, this very season can also bring about a curious paradox: spring fatigue. By tuning into nature's cues, we can better handle this seasonal dichotomy.

Adapting to natural rhythms isn't just about adjusting specific routines; it's about embracing a mindset. Imagine starting your day with a slight nod to nature—allowing the first light of sunrise to guide your waking hours. Exposure to early morning light not only sets your circadian rhythm but also positively impacts your mood.

This natural setup can be just as effective in spring as it is important in other seasons. As the days grow longer, we have more daylight to utilise, but it's crucial to balance this surge of energy with periods of rest. Allowing yourself a mindful pause in your day can combat the phenomenon of spring fatigue, ushering in both energy and tranquillity.

When we enter the heady days of summer, the extended daylight can feel almost intoxicating. Yet, this is another pivotal moment to embrace natural rhythms. Summer offers longer days—perfect for outdoor activities—but also a need for cooling down and pacing oneself. Remember, even the sun sets, giving way to rejuvenating nights.

As autumn arrives with its own set of rhythms, we are once again presented with a chance to recalibrate. This is the season of harvest, a time for both tangible and emotional gathering. Falling leaves signal a winding down, a time to prepare for the cocooning months of winter. The natural rhythm of autumn encourages us to reflect, to harvest our own experiences, and to plant seeds for future growth.

Winter, perhaps the most challenging season for many, necessitates a different approach. This quieter, more introspective time can be harnessed for self-care and reflection. Aligning with the natural rhythm of winter means surrendering to longer nights and shorter days, turning inward and focusing on restoration. Activities like light therapy can be especially effective during this time, helping to synchronize us with the limited natural light available.

Embracing natural rhythms is not a one-size-fits-all solution but rather a guidepost. Each person's seasonal response is unique, and recognising your own patterns can be a powerful tool for mental health. Journaling can be an effective way to track these changes, providing insights that are otherwise easily overlooked.

Additionally, let us not underestimate the role of diet and exercise aligned with these natural cycles. Eating seasonal foods not only nourishes the body but also connects us with the earth's innate timing. Exercise habits tailored to each season—whether outdoor jogging in spring or cosy indoor stretches in winter—help maintain our physical and emotional equilibrium.

Cultivating mindfulness and relaxation techniques, such as meditation and deep breathing, can fortify our response to seasonal changes. Techniques like these allow us to remain present, acknowledging the seasonal transitions without becoming overwhelmed by them. This conscious alignment with nature's pace encourages a balanced and fulfilling life.

Moreover, we should engage with seasonal activities that light up our spirits. In spring, gardening can be a great way to ground ourselves. Summer invites us to soak in the vibrancy of life with outdoor adventures. Autumn's cooler temperatures make it perfect for reflective walks among the falling leaves. Winter can be a time for indoor hobbies that keep our minds engaged and spirits lifted.

Social connections further bolster our well-being across the seasons. Hosting gatherings in the warm glow of summer or cozying up with friends during winter months ensures that we don't face these seasonal shifts in isolation.

To truly embrace natural rhythms is to acknowledge and flow with the cycles of energy present in each season. This harmony between our inner selves and the external world can transform seasonal mood challenges into a graceful dance with nature. Embracing these natural cues can be not just a coping mechanism but a path to thriving throughout the year.

So, let's give ourselves permission to slow down at times, speed up at others, rest, and rejuvenate as nature intends for us. By integrating these rhythms into our daily lives, we align ourselves with a balance that has been in place long before modern conveniences came into play. Embracing natural rhythms, therefore, becomes more than just a strategy—it's a lifestyle, one that respects the ancient wisdom of the earth and leads us towards a more balanced existence.

Diet and Exercise for Spring Vitality shouldn't be an afterthought; instead, it's your propulsion to welcome the season's vibrancy head-on. The paradox of renewed energy versus spring fatigue can be navigated effectively with the right dietary choices and an invigorating exercise regimen. Spring demands a different approach compared to the hibernation and comfort foods of winter. It's a season that encourages lightness, freshness, and movement.

Spring heralds an abundance of fresh produce. Incorporating seasonal fruits and vegetables into your diet can boost not just your physical health but also your mood. Think tender asparagus, zesty radishes, and sweet strawberries. These aren't just culinary delights; they're packed with vitamins and antioxidants that energise the body and mind. Leafy greens like spinach and kale, rich in folate, are known to help combat depression, making them perfect candidates for your spring salads.

Resetting your diet during spring doesn't mean you need to overhaul everything at once. Start by gradually introducing more fresh produce into your meals. A morning smoothie with spinach, a handful of berries, and a splash of almond milk can set a positive tone for your day. Lunch could be a hearty quinoa salad with mixed greens, cherry tomatoes, and cucumbers. For dinner, think grilled fish with a side of roasted spring vegetables. Simple tweaks like these can make a significant impact on your overall well-being.

As crucial as what you eat is how you eat. Spring is an ideal time to practice mindful eating. This involves paying full attention to your food—its colours, textures, and flavours—and appreciating each bite. Not only does this enhance your relationship with food, but it also helps prevent overeating and promotes better digestion.

Switching gears to exercise, spring's warmer weather and longer days are perfect invitations to take your workouts outside. There's something undeniably revitalising about exercising in the fresh air. Whether it's a brisk walk in the park, a jog along a river path, or a bike ride through blooming gardens, outdoor activities can greatly boost your mental health. The increased exposure to natural light can improve your mood and help regulate your sleep patterns, which often get disrupted during the darker winter months.

Integrating regular exercise into your spring routine doesn't have to be daunting. Start small if you need to. A 20-minute walk after dinner can serve as both exercise and a mindfulness practice. Gradually increase your activity levels as you feel more capable. Group activities such as joining a local walking or gardening club can provide the added benefit of social interaction, which in itself can be a potent mood enhancer.

Don't overlook the power of strength training in your spring fitness regimen. Incorporating bodyweight exercises such as squats, lunges, and planks can help build muscle and endurance. This is especially important as we prepare for the more active summer months ahead. You don't need a gym membership or fancy equipment; a good pair of trainers and a bit of determination can go a long way.

Spring is also a great time to revisit yoga or pilates. These practices aren't just about flexibility and strength; they're fundamentally rooted in breath work and mindfulness. Connecting breath with movement can be incredibly soothing for the mind. An outdoor yoga session, with the sounds of nature as your backdrop, can be a deeply grounding experience.

Hydration is another key aspect of spring vitality. As the temperatures climb, your body needs more fluids to function optimally. Herb-infused waters, like mint and cucumber, can make hydration more enjoyable and offer additional detoxifying benefits. Keep a water bottle with you at all times, and make it a habit to sip frequently throughout the day.

For those who struggle with spring fatigue, a balanced diet paired with regular exercise can work wonders. Fatigue often stems from a sluggish metabolism—which can be spurred into action with the right nutrients and physical activity. Foods rich in omega-3 fatty acids, like salmon and chia seeds, are known to fight inflammation and improve brain function, which can help combat that seasonal sluggishness.

Consistency is key. Building a routine that includes a mix of cardiovascular exercise, strength training, and flexibility work, paired with a nutrient-dense diet, creates a multifaceted approach to health. This isn't about quick fixes or drastic changes; it's about creating sustainable habits that keep you energised and resilient throughout the spring and beyond.

Understanding your body's response to these changes is crucial. Keep a journal to track what foods energise you, which exercises leave you feeling invigorated, and any patterns in your mood. This self-awareness can guide you in tailoring your diet and exercise plan to suit your individual needs best.

Lastly, never underestimate the power of rest and recovery. As much as spring invites us to get active, it's equally important to listen to your body and allow it to rest when needed. A balanced approach, incorporating adequate sleep and relaxation techniques such as meditation, ensures that you can enjoy all the benefits of spring without burning out.

Diet and exercise are your tools to navigate spring vitality effectively. They're not just tasks to tick off a list but elements of a lifestyle that nurture your body and mind. By embracing these practices, you're not only combating spring fatigue but also positioning yourself to fully enjoy the season's energy and vibrancy.

Chapter 3:
Summer: Brightness and Lull

As we transition from the awakening of spring to the brightness of summer, the lengthy days bring with them a unique blend of vibrancy and relaxation. The extended daylight acts like a double-edged sword: while it fills us with energy and enthusiasm, it can also lead to a sense of lethargy indistinguishable from a lull. On one hand, the sun's relentless presence lifts our spirits and encourages outdoor activity, awakening a sense of adventure and freedom. Yet, sometimes the heat can be overwhelming, causing us to retreat into the cool shade, taking refuge in moments of stillness and deep contemplation. It's during these times that our mental clarity can shine brightest, urging us to focus on self-care, embrace mindful outdoor activities, and find the perfect balance between productivity and relaxation. Understanding this dynamic helps in leveraging summer's warmth to fortify our well-being and prepare for the seasons ahead.

The Vibrancy of Summer

Summer bursts onto the scene with a vivid charm, invigorating our senses with its warmth and extended daylight. The season's energy is palpable, encouraging us to step outside, bask in the sun, and partake in nature's splendour. This period doesn't merely brighten our physical surroundings but also illuminates our inner worlds, often lifting spirits and reigniting passions. With longer days, there's more time to engage in activities that promote well-being, from early morning jogs to tranquil evening walks. However, while summer's vibrancy can be a powerful elixir for many, it's crucial to remember that the key to harnessing its full potential lies in balance. Embracing the proactive opportunities of summer while also recognising when to rest can transform this vibrant season into a cornerstone of your mental health strategy.

The Impact of Extended Daylight is often a transformative yet underappreciated aspect of the summer season. Extended daylight hours don't just affect how late we can enjoy a barbeque; they profoundly influence our mental and emotional states. Let's delve into how this added light can be harnessed to improve one's well-being.

During summer, daylight stretches well into the evening, providing ample time for activities that might be rushed or impossible during the shorter days of winter. This abundance of light triggers various physiological responses, notably in how our bodies produce melatonin, the hormone responsible for regulating sleep-wake cycles. Longer exposure to daylight delays melatonin production, often resulting in increased alertness and energy levels.

This boost in energy can be both a blessing and a challenge. Initially, the extended daylight feels like an invitation to maximise productivity and enjoy leisure activities. However, for some, this can lead to a paradoxical sense of fatigue if not managed properly. Hence, understanding how to balance this newfound energy is crucial.

One of the most significant benefits of extended daylight is its potential to alleviate symptoms of depression, particularly Seasonal Affective Disorder (SAD). The increased exposure to natural light improves serotonin production—a neurotransmitter linked to mood regulation. Consequently, individuals often experience heightened feelings of happiness and well-being.

Yet, it's not just about biological changes. Extended daylight fosters social interactions. Outdoor activities become more frequent, community events blossom, and there's an overall sense of communal vitality. These social engagements further enhance mental health by nurturing connections and reducing feelings of isolation.

Moreover, taking advantage of the extra daylight provides an excellent opportunity to incorporate exercise into daily routines. Outdoor physical activities, whether it's a simple walk, a cycling session, or a game of tennis, benefit from the longer days. Exercise, in turn, offers its own set of mental health benefits, including stress reduction and enhanced mood.

Interestingly, the quality of sleep also improves with the careful management of extended daylight. While it's easy to think the increased light might disrupt sleep patterns, following the natural cues for winding down as the sun sets can lead to a more restful sleep. Incorporating relaxation techniques like evening yoga or reading outdoors as the light dims can set a peaceful tone for the night.

Additionally, extended daylight encourages mindfulness and a deeper connection with nature. Simple activities such as gardening or walking in the park become more accessible and enjoyable. Mindfulness practices benefit from the calming effects of natural settings illuminated by longer daylight hours, making them more effective in reducing anxiety and stress.

It's crucial to address that longer days also carry a risk of overextension, where the desire to utilise every hour can lead to burnout. Therefore, setting boundaries and recognizing one's limits is essential. Planning and scheduling downtime helps maintain a healthy balance and ensures that the advantages of extended daylight aren't overshadowed by fatigue.

The influence of extended daylight extends into dietary habits as well. The longer days often encourage healthier eating patterns, with more fresh produce in season and the opportunity for outdoor meals. Maintaining a balanced diet rich in fruits and vegetables amplifies the positive effects of sunlight and boosts overall well-being.

Families can benefit by incorporating extended daylight into their routines. Engaging in evening family activities such as bike rides, picnics, or even leisurely strolls can strengthen familial bonds. These shared moments under the extended daylight reinforce emotional connectivity, providing a buffer against daily stresses.

Workplaces can also harness the benefits of extended daylight by promoting outdoor breaks and flexible hours. Encouraging employees to take lunch breaks outside, hold walking meetings, or end the workday slightly earlier to enjoy the daylight can lead to a more refreshed and productive workforce.

Beyond personal and family life, extended daylight offers a unique chance to engage in volunteer activities. Many community projects, like park clean-ups or local markets, thrive in the summer's generosity. Participation in such efforts fosters a sense of purpose and accomplishment, further boosting mental health.

Extended daylight is a powerful natural tool that, when leveraged wisely, can bring about significant positive changes in mental and emotional well-being. While it's tempting to say goodbye to productivity earlier, understanding and embracing the opportunities that come with those longer days can turn challenges into avenues for self-improvement and community engagement.

In conclusion, **The Impact of Extended Daylight** presents a remarkable opportunity for enhanced well-being. By mastering the balance between activity and rest, social interaction, and solitude, one can make the most of the summer months, turning extended daylight into a catalyst for growth and happiness.

Navigating the Summer Lull

As the initial excitement of summer's sunshine fades, many find themselves facing a surprising lull in energy and enthusiasm. Although the days are long and filled with light, it's not uncommon to feel an undercurrent of lethargy that contrasts sharply with the season's vibrant exterior. Balancing the desire to be active with the body's natural inclination to slow down in the heat can be tricky. The key to navigating this period is to listen to your body and mind, integrating cooling practices and motivational boosts as needed. Seek shaded parks for your outdoor ambitions, indulge in hydrating foods, and don't shy away from afternoon siestas. Embrace mindfulness activities like gentle yoga or meditation in the cooler parts of the day to keep your mental state balanced. Remember, summer offers a unique opportunity to cultivate a different type of energy—one that's more about sustained, mindful living than intense bursts of activity.

Staying Cool and Motivated during the summer can often feel like a test of endurance. The long, bright days that we welcome with open arms in June begin to weigh heavily on us come August. It's easy to lose momentum when the heat sets in and our routines get disrupted. But, it doesn't have to be a struggle. By adopting some practical strategies, you can not only survive the summer but thrive in it.

Firstly, let's acknowledge the energy-sapping power of high temperatures. The heat can make even the simplest tasks feel Herculean. To stay cool, consider the basics: dress in light, breathable fabrics, stay hydrated, and take breaks in the shade or indoors with a fan or air conditioning if you can. These steps might seem obvious, but they're fundamental in maintaining your energy levels.

Next, let's talk about how to keep your motivation alive. Motivation can be particularly elusive when the heat makes you feel sluggish. One effective tactic is to start your day early. Mornings are generally cooler and quieter, providing a serene environment for productivity. Early rising can give you a head start, setting a positive tone for the rest of the day.

Breaking your tasks into smaller, manageable chunks can also help sustain motivation. Instead of one long, daunting to-do list, try to tackle your responsibilities in short bursts, interspersed with cool-down periods. This method, often referred to as the Pomodoro Technique, can prevent burnout and help maintain a steady workflow.

Exercise, although it may seem counterintuitive, is crucial for staying motivated. Physical activity boosts endorphins, your body's natural mood lifters. To avoid overheating, opt for early morning or late evening workouts. Swimming, for instance, is an excellent summer exercise that's both refreshing and invigorating. Alternatively, indoor activities like yoga or a light gym session can keep you active without exposing you to extreme temperatures.

Incorporating mindfulness practices into your daily routine can also help. Mindfulness allows you to stay present and appreciative, which can combat the feelings of lethargy brought on by the heat. Simple techniques like deep breathing, meditation, or even a mindful walk can significantly impact your mental clarity and motivation levels.

One can't underestimate the power of proper nutrition in managing both the physical and mental effects of summer. Eating lighter meals more frequently helps keep your body cool and energy levels stable. Fresh fruits and vegetables, particularly those with high water content like watermelon and cucumbers, are excellent choices for staying hydrated and energised.

Let's not forget the importance of setting realistic goals during this period. It might be beneficial to adjust your expectations and deadlines to account for the slower pace brought on by summer. This doesn't mean you should lower your standards but rather be kind to yourself and acknowledge that it's okay to move at a different rhythm.

Social interactions can also be a fantastic motivator. Summer is a great time for social activities that can break the monotony of work and provide a refreshing change of pace. Whether it's a barbecue with friends, a picnic in the park, or simply a casual get-together, social engagement can rejuvenate your spirits and keep you motivated.

Engaging with nature is another powerful way to maintain motivation during summer. Being outdoors, even if it's just for a short walk in the park, can boost your mood and provide a sense of accomplishment. The vibrant colours and the liveliness of the season can be incredibly uplifting and energising.

It's also crucial to stay organised. Clutter and disorganisation can add to the feeling of chaos that the summer heat sometimes brings. Keep your workspace tidy and plan your day with clear, achievable goals. A well-organised environment can boost productivity and reduce stress.

Sleep, often neglected in the hustle and bustle of summer activities, plays a vital role in staying motivated. Ensure you're getting enough rest by creating a cool, dark sleeping environment. Proper sleep helps your body recover and recharge for the next day, maintaining your overall motivation and well-being.

Remember to take advantage of technology to help you stay cool and motivated. There are numerous apps available that can track your hydration levels, remind you to take breaks, and even guide you through mindfulness exercises. These digital tools can be great allies in managing the summer heat and maintaining your motivation.

Finally, self-compassion is key. Summer, with all its beauty and challenges, is just one part of the annual cycle. Allow yourself to ebb and flow with it, taking the necessary steps to care for your mental and physical well-being. Patience and kindness towards yourself can make a significant difference in how you experience and respond to the season's demands.

In conclusion, staying cool and motivated during the summer requires a blend of practical tactics and mindful living. By recognising the unique challenges of the season and implementing these strategies, you can turn potential obstacles into opportunities for personal growth and enjoyment. Embrace the summer not as a hurdle but as a chance to develop resilience and discover new ways to thrive.

Mindfulness and Outdoor Activities offer a robust toolkit for managing the intrinsic ups and downs of summer. The vibrancy of summer is an enigma of joy and, paradoxically, lull. Extended daylight entices us to maximise our hours, while the languor of midday heat can often lead us into a slump. Engaging mindfully in outdoor activities not only counters this lull but also enriches our overall well-being, blending physical activity with mental clarity.

First, let's dive into the essence of mindfulness. At its core, it's about being fully present in the moment, acknowledging thoughts and feelings without judgement. It might sound simple, but in practice, it entails harnessing a profound sense of awareness and connection to your surroundings. When we bring mindfulness to outdoor activities, the benefits multiply. The smell of the earth after rain, the feel of the wind against your skin, the cacophony of birds—these sensory experiences become more vivid and grounding when approached mindfully.

Consider starting your day with a mindful walk. The best part? You don't need to carve out extensive time slots; even a brief stroll can set a positive tone for the day. Focus on the act of walking itself—the rhythm of your footsteps, the shifting sounds of nature. Try to let go of any distractions. This practice, often called a "walking meditation", can help centre your thoughts and reduce anxiety.

Gardening is another activity that dovetails perfectly with mindfulness. The repetitive actions of digging, planting, and watering can become meditative practices. Being close to soil has been shown to foster a sense of accomplishment and connection to nature. It doesn't have to be an elaborate garden either; a simple potted plant on your balcony can provide a daily ritual of care and mindfulness.

Moreover, incorporating mindfulness into outdoor workouts such as yoga or tai chi can yield transformative results. These practices naturally encourage deep, mindful breathing and deliberate move-ment. When performed outdoors, the fusion of inner and outer environments heightens their calming effects. The sunlight on your face or the sound of leaves rustling becomes part of the practice, synchronising your body and mind with nature's rhythms.

Swimming in natural bodies of water, like lakes or the sea, can also become a mindful experience. Feel the buoyancy as you float, the coolness of the water against your skin. Pay attention to your strokes and breaths. The rhythmic nature of swimming can induce a meditative state, helping to calm a restless mind.

Summer is also a perfect time to explore any local parks or nature reserves that you might have been too busy to visit. Planning mindful picnics where you savour each bite, feel the grass beneath you, and listen to the ambient noises around can turn an ordinary meal into an extraordinary experience. You'll find that eating slowly and mindfully actually makes food taste better and leaves you feeling more satisfied.

For those who enjoy cycling, adding a mindful angle can transform a routine ride into a rejuvenating activity. Focus on the sensation of your muscles working, the changing landscapes, and the fresh air filling your lungs. Instead of zoning out or focusing on speed, use the ride to observe your thoughts and surroundings without rushing.

Traditional camping can be a profound way to immerse oneself in mindfulness. Disconnecting from digital devices and spending a night or two under the stars sets a natural rhythm to your days and nights. Pitching a tent, making a campfire, even cooking outside—all these tasks demand your attention and can become mindfulness practices if done with intention.

Birdwatching or simply wildlife spotting can also serve as mindful activities. They're all about observation and patience, two key pillars of mindfulness. Take a pair of binoculars, find a serene spot, and just watch. The intricate behaviours of animals and birds can be captivating, drawing your attention and calming your mind.

Joining a local outdoor mindfulness group or class can be both motivating and enriching. Many communities offer outdoor yoga sessions, group hikes, or even guided nature meditations. Sharing these experiences with others can enhance the sense of connection and provide additional support in your mindfulness journey.

Let's not overlook how children's involvement in mindful outdoor activities can be beneficial for the whole family. Encourage them to feel the textures of different leaves, listen to the sounds of different insects, and even practise basic yoga poses in the park. Such activities can help foster a lifelong appreciation for nature and mindfulness.

Acknowledge that mindfulness is a practice and, like all practices, requires patience and persistence. The results are often subtle and gradual but undeniably powerful. As you continue to incorporate mindfulness into your outdoor activities, you'll likely find not just a reduction in the summer lull but an enhancement in your overall quality of life.

In the end, the key to unlocking the full potential of summer doesn't lie in overloading your to-do list. Instead, it's about finding balance and presence in each activity. Through mindful engagement with the natural world, we can rejuvenate our bodies and calm our minds, turning every summer day into an opportunity for renewal and joy.

Chapter 4:
Autumn: Harvest and Depression

Autumn, with its tapestry of amber and crimson, presents a juxtaposition of abundance and melancholy. While this season often brings the joy of harvest, a time to celebrate the fruits of our labour and prepare for the colder months ahead, it also ushers in a wave of introspection and, for many, a struggle with low spirits. The crisp air and shortening days can serve as trigger factors for autumn depression, known to some as "the autumn blues". It's vital to understand and address the reasons behind these feelings. On one hand, the natural decline in daylight can disrupt our circadian rhythms and affect our mood. On the other, the transition period offers a unique opportunity to create comfort and forge connections that bolster mental health. By acknowledging autumn's dual nature, we can adopt strategies that turn this season into a time of inner harvest as well, focusing on self-awareness, warmth, and community. Engaging in activities like hearty cooking, cosy gatherings, and reflective journaling can transform the descent of autumn into an ascent of personal growth and well-being, setting a foundation for the winter months.

Autumn's Dual Nature

Autumn captures the essence of life's duality. It's a season of bright oranges, deep reds, and golden yellows, symbolising the richness of harvest and the impending quiet of winter. Yet, alongside the splendour, many find themselves buckling under the weight of melancholy. It's as if the beauty carries a hint of sorrow, whispering that the days are getting shorter and the warmth is slipping away. For those affected by seasonal mood variations, understanding this dual nature is key. Recognising that autumn holds both the promise of abundance and the spectre of depression can be empowering. This awareness allows us to harness its potential for growth while arming ourselves with strategies to stave off the blues. In essence, acknowledging autumn's duality helps us prepare emotionally for winter, ensuring the season serves as a time for reflection and inner harvest rather than unchecked despondency.

Harvest Time and Preparing for Winter are a significant aspect of autumn's dual nature. As the days shorten and the air crisps, nature signals us to slow down and gather the bounty of the season. This transition period, if handled thoughtfully, can prepare us mentally and physically for the cold months ahead.

During harvest time, the landscape is awash with change. The trees blaze with fiery hues, and the crops beg to be collected. For centuries, harvest has been synonymous with abundance and gratitude. It's a time when communities come together to celebrate the fruits of the year's labour. Applying this tradition can be hugely beneficial for our mental health as we embrace a sense of gratitude and community.

One of the best ways to emotionally and mentally transition into winter is by leaning into the act of harvesting. Whether you're picking apples, gathering vegetables from your garden, or simply spending time in nature, these activities root you in the present moment. This seasonal mindfulness can anchor you, helping to ward off the encroaching gloom that can accompany autumn's shorter days.

Early autumn is also the perfect time to assess your surroundings and prepare for the indoor months. Begin by organising your living space to ensure it is both cosy and functional. If possible, introduce elements of nature into your home. Think along the lines of dried flowers, autumnal wreaths, and even the earthy scents of pine cones and cinnamon. This physical preparation can give a psychological lift, creating a sanctuary where you can retreat during winter.

Diet plays a crucial role in how we feel as we head into winter. With the harvest in full swing, it's an excellent time to savour seasonal produce. Root vegetables, squash, and leafy greens are not only comforting but packed with nutrients that support mental well-being. Think hearty soups, stews, and roasted vegetables. These warm, nourishing dishes can be a form of self-care, providing the comfort and energy necessary to face colder days.

While our ancestors prepared for winter out of necessity, we can adopt their practices for our mental readiness. Canning, preserving, and storing foods create a literal and figurative sense of security. Stocking up your pantry or freezing the harvest's bounty can offer a feeling of stability and preparedness, key for maintaining a positive outlook through the darker months.

Exercise may not be top of mind during colder weeks, but integrating a regular regime can significantly impact your mood. Autumn's cool air and scenic beauty make it the ideal time for outdoor activities—hiking, gentle walks, or even bike rides. These activities not only help keep your body fit but also allow you to soak up the last of the seasonal daylight, crucial for staving off the autumnal blues.

An integral piece of preparing for winter is acknowledging and respecting the natural slowing down of the season. Just as trees shed their leaves to conserve energy, it's necessary for us to adjust our pace. This doesn't mean giving in to lethargy but rather finding a balance between restful activities and those that invigorate. Practising yoga, engaging in light reading, or enjoying arts and crafts can be soothing alternatives to high-energy exercises.

Mental preparation for winter cannot overlook the importance of social connections. As we harvest and prepare, it's beneficial to foster relationships. Sharing meals, joining community events, or even virtual gatherings can fortify our mental defences against the isolating tendencies of winter. Human connection acts as a buffer, providing emotional warmth and stability.

Deep cleaning and decluttering are often associated with spring but can be equally beneficial in autumn. This task goes beyond cleanliness—a neat, organised space can reduce stress and enhance mental clarity. By creating an orderly environment, you're setting the stage for a mentally calmer winter. It can be cathartic to let go of items that no longer serve you, making room for new experiences and opportunities.

Participating in or creating rituals can amplify the sense of transition and readiness. Simple yet effective rituals—lighting candles, enjoying a special tea, or listening to seasonal music—create markers in your routine that denote change. These small acts can enrich the daily monotony and provide comfort and structure, essential during less active seasons.

There's an undeniable power in seasonal storytelling and literature. Dive into books that highlight autumn themes or folklore. These stories often resonate with our inherent connection to the season, offering both entertainment and an emotional roadmap. Reading can be a delightful escape and a way to internalise autumn's teachings.

Sustaining your mental health as you prepare for winter involves a holistic approach. It's about combining the physical tasks of harvest with emotional readiness. Embrace autumn's gifts and use them to fortify yourself against the challenges of the upcoming cold season. This blend of tradition, mindfulness, and community can set the stage for a positive and fulfilling seasonal cycle.

Technological aids, such as lightboxes and sunrise alarm clocks, can also be part of your preparatory toolkit. These devices can mitigate the impact of reduced daylight and help regulate your circadian rhythms. Incorporating technology thoughtfully can provide the extra support you need as natural light wanes.

The beauty of harvest time in preparing for winter lies in its simplicity and connection to nature. By tuning into what nature offers, aligning your habits, and fostering relationships, you can transform what seems like a period of decline into an opportunity for enrichment. A well-prepared mind and body can thrive, even when the external environment challenges us.

Facing Autumn Depression

As the days grow shorter and the vibrant summer gradually yields to autumn's crisp embrace, feelings of melancholy can start to seep in. This seasonal shift, often marked by gloomy skies and falling leaves, has a profound effect on our emotional landscape. If you're feeling the weight of autumn depression, it's essential to first acknowledge and understand it as a natural response to the changing environment. Take this time to create comfort and foster connections; light candles, enjoy warm beverages, and envelop yourself in cosy blankets. Engaging in activities that bring joy and leaning on social support can make a significant difference. Remember, this isn't just about braving the storm—it's about finding ways to thrive amidst it.

Understanding the Trigger Factors is crucial in grasping the underlying causes of autumnal mood shifts. Autumn, with its falling leaves and shorter days, often brings a sense of reflection and introspection. While this season has a certain poetic charm, it can also evoke feelings of sadness and lethargy, sometimes leading to what's commonly known as autumn depression. To navigate this period effectively, we need to pinpoint what triggers these mood changes.

The first and most apparent trigger is the reduction in daylight hours. During autumn, the days gradually become shorter, leading to extended periods of darkness. This lack of natural light can disrupt our circadian rhythms, which in turn affects the production of melatonin and serotonin—two hormones crucial for regulating sleep and mood respectively.

Beyond the physical impact of decreased daylight, psychological factors also play a significant role. Autumn is often associated with the coming of winter—a season many perceive as daunting or oppressive. This anticipation can create a mental burden, inducing anxiety and stress over the impending cold months and the lifestyle adjustments required to cope with them.

Furthermore, there are social and cultural triggers to consider. Autumn frequently marks the beginning of the school year and the end of summer holidays. This return to routine and increased responsibilities can generate stress. Children and adults alike may feel overwhelmed by the sudden shift from a relaxed summer pace to the rigorous demands of work and school schedules.

Another prevalent trigger is the connection between autumn and certain anniversaries or memories. For many, autumn might be the season of personal loss or significant life changes, such as moving to a new city for educational or professional reasons. These memories can resurface, causing emotional turbulence and contributing to a melancholic state.

Food and diet also play an influential role during this time. As the weather cools, people tend to crave comfort foods, which are often high in sugars and carbohydrates. Although these foods offer immediate pleasure, they can lead to "sugar crashes" and ultimately dampen one's mood. Lack of fresh produce during autumn may also result in nutritional deficiencies, exacerbating feelings of tiredness and depression.

Economic factors shouldn't be overlooked either. The onset of autumn typically heralds higher expenses related to heating homes, purchasing winter clothing, and holiday preparations. The financial strain can be a substantial source of stress, particularly for those already managing tight budgets.

Furthermore, seasonal allergies are another often-neglected trigger. During autumn, various allergens like mould spores and ragweed pollen are prevalent. Allergic reactions can mimic or exacerbate symptoms of depression, such as fatigue and irritability. Understanding this link can help in finding appropriate treatments, alleviating unnecessary discomfort.

Exercise patterns are affected too. Many people reduce their outdoor activities as temperatures drop, leading to less physical exercise which in turn affects overall mood and energy levels. The lack of physical activity can diminish endorphin production, those delightful hormones that make us feel good after a brisk walk or jog.

The social calendar in autumn changes as well. With fewer festivals and outdoor gatherings, there's often a decline in social interactions. This increase in isolation can compound feelings of loneliness and depression. Emphasising alternative social engagements or indoor activities can help mitigate this trigger.

Moreover, not all triggers are overtly negative. Seasonal affective disorder (SAD) is a condition that significantly impacts some individuals during the autumn months. Although the exact cause is still under research, it's believed to be linked to changes in light exposure. The understanding and acknowledgment of SAD as a genuine health issue can be empowering for those affected, providing a pathway to effective treatments like light therapy.

Lastly, it's worth mentioning the emotional complexity of this season. Autumn carries an inherent duality; the beauty of changing leaves and harvests stands in stark contrast to the decline in temperatures and daylight. This duality can make individuals feel conflicted, enjoying the aesthetics of the season while grappling with internal emotional shifts.

Ultimately, recognising these trigger factors is a vital step towards crafting effective strategies to combat autumn depression. Whether it involves adjusting daily routines to include more exposure to natural light, managing responsibilities to minimise stress, or understanding the importance of social connections, informed action can transform potential challenges into opportunities for growth and well-being.

Knowledge is power. By understanding the various triggers of autumnal mood shifts, you're better equipped to anticipate and mitigate their effects. Taking proactive steps not only enhances your mental health but also enriches your experience of this beautiful, albeit complex, season.

Creating Comfort and Connection during autumn is essential to keep seasonal mood variations at bay and promote overall well-being. As the leaves change colour and the air becomes crisper, many people start to feel an undercurrent of melancholy or anxiety. It's crucial to acknowledge these feelings and actively seek ways to combat them.

The shift from long, sun-drenched days to shorter, darker ones can be jarring. We need to consciously create an environment that offers comfort and fosters connections. The first step in this direction is to make our living spaces warm and inviting. Think about integrating soft lighting, cosy blankets, and seasonal decorations. A well-lit room with aromatic candles can significantly elevate one's mood.

But it's not just about physical comfort. Emotional comfort is equally important. Autumn can be a time to re-evaluate and deepen our relationships. It's easy to feel isolated as the days grow shorter, but reaching out to friends and family can build a support network that provides emotional sustenance. A simple phone call or a shared cup of tea can work wonders.

When it comes to creating connection, think about activities that can be enjoyed together. A book club, autumn crafts, or even a seasonal cooking class can be excellent ways to stay engaged and connected. These activities not only provide a distraction but also foster a sense of community.

Regular gatherings, however small, are crucial in battling the loneliness that can come with autumn's more introspective nature. Hosting a potluck dinner or a film night can create a warm, inclusive atmosphere, making people feel supported and less isolated.

Pets can also offer a unique form of comfort and connection. The unconditional love and companionship of a pet can relieve stress and provide emotional stability. Consider spending more time with your furry friends. Their companionship often acts as a grounding force.

Equally important is connecting with nature. Autumn's beauty is unparalleled, and taking time to appreciate it can have a grounding effect. Walks in the park, hikes in the woods, or even a visit to a local orchard can create a peaceful yet exhilarating experience. Nature walks have been shown to reduce stress and improve overall well-being.

Community involvement tends to dip as we head into autumn, but staying socially active is essential. Volunteering at local events or joining community groups can provide a sense of purpose and belonging. Plus, helping others often reduces our own feelings of helplessness or sadness.

Let's not overlook the role of self-care routines in creating comfort. Pamper yourself with warm baths, skincare routines, or even a good book. These small acts of self-care can accumulate to create a cocoon of comfort, helping to fend off the seasonal blues.

A consistent sleep schedule also plays a pivotal role in maintaining mental health. As the nights grow longer, it becomes easier to fall into irregular sleep patterns. Aligning your sleep with the natural rhythm of the season can make a substantial difference in how you feel.

Dealing with the shift in weather can also mean adjusting your wardrobe. Wearing layers and comfortable clothing helps keep you physically warm, contributing to a general sense of well-being. It's surprising how much difference woollen socks or a favourite jumper can make.

Music and aromatherapy are other tools that can enhance your emotional environment. Playlists of your favourite songs or ambient sounds, combined with scents like lavender or eucalyptus, can create a calming atmosphere. Small efforts in sensory engagement can significantly flatten the emotional ups and downs.

Autumn is also an excellent time to embark on creative projects. Whether it's painting, knitting, or writing, creative activities can be incredibly therapeutic. They allow for self-expression and provide a focus away from negative thoughts or anxieties.

Physical exercise must not be sidelined either. While the dropping temperatures might make one hesitant to work out, exercising helps elevate your mood. Indoor activities like yoga or dance can offer both physical benefits and a sense of accomplishment.

The season of harvest is ultimately an opportunity to harvest our relationships, inner strength, and communal bonds. By actively seeking out comfort and nurtured connections, we turn autumn from a time of potential depression into a season of flourishing connections and emotional warmth.

Chapter 5:
Winter: Chills and Blues

Winter, with its quiet embrace, often feels like nature's pause button. The chill in the air can bring a sense of stillness, encouraging us to slow down and reflect, but this same stillness can also invite the winter blues. While some find solace in this period of introspection, others struggle with the reduced daylight and colder temperatures, which can dampen our spirits. It's a season of contrasts, where the beauty of snow-covered landscapes can mask the internal chill some of us feel. Thankfully, there are ways to navigate these challenges and turn the chilly gloom into an opportunity for growth and renewal. By incorporating light therapy, fostering social connections, and engaging in seasonal activities, we can beat the blues and uncover the hidden warmth winter has to offer.

The Quiet of Winter

Amidst winter's chill, a profound stillness emerges that offers unique opportunities for reflection and restoration. The landscape, draped in blankets of snow, seems to whisper for us to slow down and take stock of our internal world. This season is not just about enduring the darkness but embracing the calm it brings, a calm that allows us to listen to our own thoughts and emotions more deeply. It's a chance to recharge, to delve into introspection, and to fortify our mental resilience. By embracing the quiet of winter, we can uncover hidden strengths and prepare ourselves mentally and emotionally for the brighter days ahead.

Reflection and Restoration often become pivotal themes as we delve into winter. As autumn's vibrant hues fade and daylight diminishes, we may find ourselves turning inward, both metaphorically and literally. The very essence of winter invites a period of stillness, where reflection and restoration are not merely encouraged but necessary.

Winter's quiet can be a powerful ally in self-reflection. During these months, the external world slows down, and so should we. It's a period to take stock of the past months, to ponder over achievements and setbacks, and to set intentions for the future. This is not about making grandiose New Year's resolutions; instead, it's about gentle introspection and compassionate goal-setting. Consider keeping a journal to document your thoughts. Penning down insights and experiences offers clarity that often goes unnoticed in the hustle of warmer months.

Restoration during winter isn't just about physical rest, although that's undoubtedly important. It's about holistic replenishment—nurturing the mind, body, and soul. Our bodies naturally crave more rest during this period, responding to the shortened days and cooler temperatures. Listen to these cues. Allowing oneself extra sleep can be rejuvenating. Ensuring you're getting quality rest is vital for maintaining mental health, helping ward off the infamous winter blues or seasonal affective disorder (SAD).

Incorporate practices that promote mental restoration. Meditation and mindfulness can be particularly beneficial during the winter months. Practising mindfulness helps ground us, bringing our awareness to the present moment, reducing anxiety and promoting a sense of inner peace. Winter is the ideal time to establish or deepen a meditation practice. Even a few minutes a day can have profound effects on your mood and overall well-being.

Physical activity also plays a crucial role in restoration, even when the chill in the air might tempt you to stay indoors. Exercise releases endorphins, our body's natural mood lifters, and helps fend off the sedentary traps of winter. Consider activities suited to the season—perhaps yoga by a cosy fire, indoor swimming, or even brisk walks on crisp, sunny days. The key is consistency over intensity. Gentle, regular movement is more sustainable and beneficial during this season.

This season also invites us to slow down and enjoy moments of stillness—a typically rare commodity in today's fast-paced world. You might find solace in simple pleasures: reading a good book, enjoying a warm cup of tea, or savouring the silence of a snowy evening. Relearning to find joy in small, quiet moments can be restorative in itself, offering a counterbalance to the over-stimulation that often characterises other times of the year.

Nutrition cannot be overlooked when discussing restoration. Our diet directly impacts our mood and energy levels. Winter calls for warming, nourishing foods that are both comforting and sustaining. Embrace seasonal vegetables like root crops and squashes; they ground us, providing the nutrients needed to support our body's natural rhythm. Soups, stews, and herbal teas can also offer both physical warmth and nutritional benefits, vital for combating the lethargy that the season may bring.

Social connections, although sometimes more challenging to maintain in winter, are crucial for emotional health. Isolation can exacerbate feelings of despondency; hence, making an effort to stay connected with loved ones is important. Whether it's a phone call, virtual meeting, or a small gathering, these interactions offer a sense of community and mutual restoration. Consider organising regular get-togethers, even if they're virtual, to foster a sense of continuity and support.

When pondering restoration, let's remember that creating a comforting environment in our living spaces can greatly enhance our mood and sense of well-being. This might involve incorporating elements of hygge, a Danish concept that revolves around creating a warm, inviting atmosphere. Think cosy blankets, candles, and calming music. The goal is to create a sanctuary where you can unwind and restore your energy levels.

Reflection also involves letting go of what's no longer serving us. This might mean decluttering your physical space or addressing emotional baggage. Both can be remarkably freeing and allow for a sense of renewal. Winter's aura of introspection makes it an ideal time for such activities.

Moreover, consider engaging in creative activities. Painting, knitting, writing, or any form of artistic expression can serve as a therapeutic outlet. Creativity allows for the expression of emotions and thoughts that might be difficult to articulate otherwise. It can be an incredibly restorative practice, fostering a sense of accomplishment and fulfillment.

Spiritual reflection may also play a part in your journey through winter. Whether through religious practices, spiritual readings, or simply spending time in nature, finding ways to connect with something larger than ourselves can provide comfort and perspective. Embrace whatever spiritually elevates you as part of your restorative practice.

Finally, planning for the future can be a form of restoration. Use this reflective period to set gentle, achievable goals. Winter is the season for introspection and planning, while more dynamic actions can follow in the coming months. Allow yourself to dream, even in the stillness, about what you want to achieve in the brighter days ahead.

In summary, **reflection and restoration** during winter embrace a holistic approach. By combining physical rest, mental introspection, social connections, and creative expression, we can navigate the challenges of the season and emerge not only restored but also prepared for the rejuvenation of spring. Use this time wisely to cultivate practices that nourish, heal, and inspire.

Combatting the Winter Blues

When winter's chill starts to seep not just into our bones but also into our spirits, it's time to roll up our sleeves and take action. Combatting the winter blues requires a multi-faceted approach. One of the most effective strategies is utilising light therapy, simulating the natural sunlight our bodies crave but often lack during the darker months. Additionally, surrounding yourself with warmth doesn't just mean cranking up the thermostat—consider cosy blankets, warm baths, and even the emotional warmth that comes from social support. Connecting with friends and family through seasonal activities, whether it's ice skating, movie marathons, or simply hearty conversations over a cup of hot chocolate, can significantly lift your mood. Winter might be quiet and still, but it doesn't mean our lives have to hit the pause button. Actively embracing simple pleasures and staying socially engaged will help keep those winter blues at bay.

Light Therapy and Warmth carry a profound significance in tackling the winter blues, a period when days are short, nights are long, and the sun often plays hide and seek. For many, winter's harsh reality can lead to a palpable lack of energy and a drop in mood. However, harnessing the power of light and warmth can turn this bleak scenario into an opportunity for rejuvenation and positive change.

First, let's dive into light therapy. Scientifically known as phototherapy, this method involves exposure to artificial light that mimics natural sunlight. It's not just a mere substitute but a therapeutic tool that can alleviate the symptoms of Seasonal Affective Disorder (SAD) and other mood fluctuations associated with the lack of sunlight during winter. Sitting in front of a lightbox each morning can reset your circadian rhythms, the body's internal clock that dictates sleep patterns and mood.

A typical light therapy session requires about 20 to 30 minutes daily. The light must be around 10,000 lux—a measure of light intensity—positioned at a comfortable distance from your face. Although the process might seem straightforward, consistency is key. Making it a part of your morning routine can set a positive tone for the day.

It's essential to consult a healthcare provider before starting light therapy. They can provide guidance on choosing the correct lightbox and ensure it's suitable for your specific needs. This simple yet effective method has gained popularity for its ability to yield powerful results, often within a few days to a couple of weeks.

Moving on to warmth, it's not merely physical comfort we're discussing but a holistic sense of well-being. Colder temperatures can lead to the urge to hibernate, which, while natural, can sometimes contribute to feelings of isolation and depression. A strategic use of warmth can counteract these tendencies, creating an inviting environment that soothes and uplifts.

One of the most delightful ways to introduce warmth is through simple daily rituals. For instance, consider incorporating a warm bath into your evening routine. The heat helps to relax muscles, reduce stress, and even promote better sleep. Adding essential oils like lavender or eucalyptus can amplify these benefits, offering both physical and mental relaxation.

A warm environment isn't solely about heating your home. It can be enhanced by the right clothing and layering. An investment in quality, cosy attire can profoundly affect your mood and comfort level. Think of soft, thermal fabrics and warm woollen socks—simple touches that create a cocoon of comfort.

Don't overlook the power of warm beverages. A cup of herbal tea or hot chocolate can be a source of tangible solace. Beyond the immediate warmth, such practices encourage moments of mindfulness, giving you a chance to pause, reflect, and recalibrate.

Heating devices like electric blankets or underfloor heating can elevate your living space, making it a sanctuary away from the cold outside. If these aren't within your reach, heating pads or hot water bottles can be affordable yet effective alternatives. They are perfect for warming your bed or snuggling with while reading a book or watching a favourite series.

Now, let's contemplate the combined effects of light therapy and warmth. On their own, they offer substantial benefits, but when integrated, they can considerably transform your winter experience. Picture starting your day with a session of light therapy, followed by wrapping yourself in a warm robe or enjoying a steaming cup of tea. It blends the best of both worlds—invigorating light to jumpstart your day and enveloping warmth to maintain a sense of comfort and security.

Engaging in outdoor activities can also amplify these benefits. On milder days, taking a brisk walk in natural light, even if it's overcast, can have a dual effect: stimulating both body and mind. Remember to wear layers to stay warm, ensuring that neither cold nor discomfort deters your commitment to these healthful practices.

Indoor exercises like yoga or stretching routines performed under a broad-spectrum lamp can further boost your mood. Combining physical activity with light exposure maximises the benefits for your mental and physical health. It's a holistic approach to embracing the otherwise challenging winter months.

Creating a warm and inviting environment isn't solely about temperature. It extends to your entire home ambiance. Think of lighting candles, using warming scents like cinnamon and vanilla, and incorporating plush textiles into your living space. These touches contribute to a sensory experience that can uplift and comfort.

Social warmth, too, should not be underestimated. Gathering with friends and family for meals, game nights, or simply enjoying each other's company can provide emotional warmth that combats the cold distance of winter. Building and maintaining these connections are vital for emotional well-being.

When crafting your winter strategy, make it personal. Select elements of light therapy and warmth that resonate most with you. This tailored approach ensures you're not merely enduring the season but truly embracing it.

In sum, light therapy and warmth aren't just remedies for winter woes; they're transformative tools that can empower you to face the season head-on. By understanding and implementing these strategies, you can turn winter from a time of struggle into a period of discovery, solace, and personal growth.

Social Support and Seasonal Activities become paramount during winter when the world seemingly slows down under a blanket of cold and gloom. It's easy to feel isolated and withdrawn during these months, which can exacerbate feelings of loneliness and sadness. However, recognising the power of social interactions, combined with engaging seasonal activities, can dramatically shift the way you experience winter, making it a time of connection and joy.

The importance of social support during this season cannot be overstated. Human beings are inherently social creatures; our mental well-being is deeply connected to our interactions with others. When confined indoors due to inclement weather, it's crucial to make a conscious effort to reach out and maintain these connections. Whether it's through planned gatherings, spontaneous coffee dates, or digital meetups via video calls, maintaining regular contact with loved ones can act as an anchor, providing emotional stability during the cold months.

Organising a winter get-together can be remarkably effective in lifting spirits. Small gestures like inviting friends over for a cosy dinner, arranging a movie night, or even hosting a themed party can encourage social engagement. Potluck dinners are a fantastic way to share not just food, but also stories, laughter, and companionship. If you're lacking inspiration, consider creating a 'winter warm-up' invite, encouraging guests to bring their favourite warming dish and a heartfelt story to share.

Moreover, focusing on community events can also help bridge the gap. Local churches, community centres, and libraries often host winter-themed events, ranging from craft fairs to winter hikes. These events provide opportunities to meet new people who are also seeking warmth and connection. You don't have to be a social butterfly to benefit from these interactions; even brief, positive encounters can uplift your mood.

Seasonal activities, tailored to winter's unique charms, play a significant role in maintaining mental wellness. Engaging in activities that embrace the winter season can change your perspective, converting what might feel like a dreary slog into an adventure. Activities like ice skating, sledging, and building snowmen can be delightful for families and friends alike. If the thought of outdoor activities sends a shiver down your spine, indoor activities such as board games, baking, or trying out new recipes can be equally fulfilling.

Incorporating light physical exercise in your winter routine can enhance mood and social connectivity. Joining a winter sports league, such as indoor football or joining a local gym for group classes, not only provides physical benefits but also fosters a sense of community. Just remember to pace yourself and choose activities that you genuinely enjoy to ensure consistency and long-term participation.

An often-overlooked aspect of social support is the mutual benefit derived from helping others. Volunteering is a powerful tool to combat winter blues. Whether it's helping at a local soup kitchen, participating in community clean-ups, or offering your time at nursing homes, the act of giving has a profound impact on your mental state. By focusing on the needs of others, you inadvertently uplift your own spirits and contribute to the well-being of your community.

Social media, while sometimes blamed for increasing feelings of isolation, can be a double-edged sword if used wisely. It can be a platform for creating and maintaining meaningful connections. Engaging in online groups and communities dedicated to winter activities can provide inspiration and interaction. Sharing your own experiences and reading about others' can serve as a reminder that you are not alone in navigating the challenges of winter.

Don't forget the simple yet powerful act of checking in on your neighbours. A small gesture, such as bringing a neighbour a homemade pie or offering to shovel their driveway, can foster a kind of neighbourhood camaraderie that creates a supportive environment for everyone. These acts remind us all of the importance of looking out for one another, especially during times that might otherwise feel isolating.

Exploring new hobbies or picking up old ones can also pave the way for new social interactions. Winter is an excellent time to enrol in a class or workshop. Whether it's painting, knitting, or even learning a new language, such activities not only keep your mind engaged but also provide a shared interest to bond over with new acquaintances. The sense of accomplishment from mastering a new skill can further elevate your mood and sense of purpose.

It's important to not overlook the simpler, quieter forms of social support. Sometimes, the mere act of sharing a quiet space with another person, even if it's through a shared reading session or a contemplative walk in the snow, can be immensely comforting. The silent companionship of someone you trust can be just as valuable as animated conversations.

For those struggling to extend their social network, joining interest-based groups and clubs can be beneficial. Many towns and cities have clubs for every conceivable interest, from book clubs and hiking groups to winter photography collectives. These are platforms where you can meet like-minded individuals in a relaxed setting, fostering both creativity and connection.

Formal support groups can also provide a lifeline. These groups, often facilitated by mental health professionals, offer a safe space to share experiences and coping strategies. The shared understanding and encouragement found in support groups can be extraordinarily reaffirming, especially for those battling seasonal affective disorder or other winter-related mood changes.

Finally, remember that it's perfectly okay to seek professional help if you find that social activities and support networks aren't enough to counteract the seasonal downs. Therapists and counsellors can provide personalised strategies and interventions that cater to your specific needs. These professionals can help navigate the complexities of seasonal mood variations and offer both solace and actionable advice.

In harnessing the power of social support and seasonal activities, winter can transform from a period of isolation into a season ripe with opportunities for deepened connections and enriching experiences. It's all about shifting perspective, embracing the season's unique offerings, and reaching out – both for help and to help others. Let's make winter not just a time to endure, but a period to thrive.

Chapter 6:
Mood Management Throughout the Seasons

Mood management throughout the seasons isn't just a matter of surviving the highs and lows; it's about turning each season's unique qualities into opportunities for growth and well-being. Understanding the role of diet is essential, as certain foods can boost your mood, helping you feel your best all year round. Exercise, too, plays a critical role, with different activities suited to different seasonal contexts – perhaps a brisk walk in winter or swimming in the height of summer. Sleep, often overlooked, should be aligned with seasonal changes to help keep your internal clock in harmony. Cultivating mindfulness and relaxation through meditation or breathing techniques can also assist in maintaining emotional balance. By integrating these practical strategies into your daily life, you can navigate seasonal mood variations not as obstacles, but as natural cycles that offer unique opportunities for self-improvement and mental wellness.

The Role of Diet in Mood Management

As the seasons change, our bodies experience shifts that can profoundly impact our mood and mental health, making diet a crucial element of our overall well-being. Research suggests that certain foods can either boost our mood or exacerbate negative feelings, depending on our dietary choices. Aligning your diet with seasonal needs can provide the necessary nutrients to support mental equilibrium. Fresh, leafy greens and berries in spring, hydrating fruits and cooling salads in summer, hearty root vegetables and nuts in autumn, and warm soups and slow-cooked stews in winter can help nourish the body and mind. Nutrient-dense foods rich in omega-3 fatty acids, vitamins, and minerals can act as natural mood enhancers, promoting the production of feel-good neurotransmitters like serotonin and dopamine. By thoughtfully choosing our meals, we create an internal environment that supports resilience and positivity, making the seasonal transitions smoother and more enjoyable.

Foods That Boost Your Mood are an essential component in the quest to maintain mental health throughout the seasons. If you've ever found yourself reaching for comfort food when you're down or noticing a spring in your step after eating something healthy, you're already aware of how powerful diet can be in affecting mood. Let's delve into how specific foods can lift your spirits and keep you balanced year-round.

First and foremost, let's talk about *complex carbohydrates*. Unlike their simple counterparts, such as sugary snacks and white bread, complex carbohydrates—found in foods like whole grains, legumes, and vegetables—provide a steady supply of glucose to the brain. This stabilises blood sugar levels, preventing the mood swings often associated with rapid spikes and drops. Consuming oatmeal, for example, can be a great way to start the day with a mood boost.

Then, there's the power of *omega-3 fatty acids*. Found predominantly in fatty fish like salmon, mackerel, and sardines, as well as flaxseeds and walnuts, omega-3s play a vital role in brain function and structure. They've been shown to reduce symptoms of depression and anxiety, making them a must in your diet, particularly when daylight hours are shorter, and your mood might naturally dip.

Speaking of brain function, let's not overlook *B vitamins*. High levels of folate, B6, and B12 are particularly important for maintaining mental health. They assist in the production of neurotransmitters like serotonin and dopamine, which are crucial for mood regulation. Leafy greens, meats, and dairy products are excellent sources of these vitamins. Don't hesitate to add a spinach salad or a serving of chicken to your daily meals.

One can't ignore the profound impact of *antioxidants*—these warriors combat oxidative stress in the brain, which is linked to mood disorders. Fruits like blueberries, strawberries, and oranges are rich in antioxidants, specifically vitamin C and flavonoids. Including a variety of colourful fruits in your diet offers an easy, tasty form of mood enhancement.

Ready for a dose of happiness? Enter *tryptophan*, an essential amino acid that your body converts into serotonin. Foods rich in tryptophan, like turkey, eggs, and cheese, can directly improve mood. This makes it a great idea to include an egg breakfast or a turkey sandwich in your day, elevating your serotonin levels naturally.

Fermented foods like yogurt, kefir, and kimchi bring gut health into the spotlight. The gut-brain connection is increasingly recognised in scientific communities, indicating that a healthy gut contributes to a healthy mind. Fermented foods increase the diversity of gut microbes, which in turn, enhances mental health. Incorporating a daily dose of probiotics through these foods can truly transform your mood.

On the topic of mental energy, *magnesium* should not be overlooked. Magnesium helps to reduce anxiety and improve sleep, two crucial components for maintaining a good mood. Sources include leafy greens, nuts, seeds, and whole grains. A handful of almonds or a spinach smoothie can go a long way in keeping your spirits up.

Hydration also deserves its moment in the spotlight. Sometimes, what feels like sadness or fatigue can actually be dehydration. Drinking enough water throughout the day is fundamental, and drinking herbal teas like chamomile or peppermint can also provide a soothing effect on your mood. Remember, your brain is composed of about 75% water, and even slight dehydration can have noticeable effects on both mood and cognitive function.

Let's not forget *dark chocolate*, an indulgence that doesn't just taste good but also makes you feel good. Rich in flavonoids and possessing a decent magnesium content, dark chocolate can decrease stress hormones and increase serotonin levels. A small piece of dark chocolate (preferably 70% cocoa or higher) can be a guilt-free treat to enhance your day.

An essential mineral, *zinc*, plays a significant role in mood regulation. Low levels of zinc have been correlated with depression, making it important to consume zinc-rich foods like beef, chickpeas, and pumpkin seeds. A simple snack of roasted pumpkin seeds or hummus can help maintain optimal zinc levels.

Don't underestimate the mood-boosting power of a good cup of *coffee or green tea*. Coffee contains caffeine that sharpens focus and boosts mood by increasing dopamine levels. Green tea, with its lower caffeine content and high levels of the amino acid L-theanine, provides a calm alertness, enhancing both mood and concentration. Sipping on these beverages can be a delightful way to improve your mood without overreliance.

Speaking of amino acids, *theanine* found in green tea can improve focus and reduce stress. It's why green tea drinkers often report a more calm and focused state of mind. Incorporating green tea into your routine can be a simple way to infuse your day with a sense of calm and clarity.

Finally, a word on *vitamin D*. Often called the "sunshine vitamin," its deficiency is linked to mood disorders, especially during the darker months. While sunlight is the best source, vitamin D can also be found in fortified foods like milk, orange juice, and cereals, as well as in fatty fish. Ensuring you get enough vitamin D can make a significant difference in your overall mood and energy levels.

Incorporating these foods into your diet doesn't have to be overwhelming. Small, deliberate changes can lead to significant improvements in your mood over time. Think of this endeavour as an opportunity to explore new recipes and ingredients, transforming your kitchen into a sanctuary of well-being. Remember, food is not just fuel; it's a cornerstone of our mental health, offering a delicious pathway to a brighter, more stable mood throughout the year.

Exercise as a Tool for Mental Health

Exercise isn't just a physical endeavour; it's a crucial component for mental health, especially when navigating mood fluctuations throughout the seasons. As natural light wanes in autumn and winter or as energy spikes in the spring and summer, purposeful movement can act as a consistent anchor, stabilising emotional highs and lows. Regular physical activity prompts the release of endorphins—also known as 'feel-good' hormones—which can alleviate symptoms of depression and anxiety, offering a natural boost to your mood. It's about discovering the right type of exercise for each season, be it invigorating walks in the crisp autumn air, cosy indoor yoga during winter, vibrant outdoor sports in summer, or refreshing runs amidst the blossoming spring scenery. Engaging in seasonal activities not only keeps your body agile but also provides a rhythmic, grounding experience that taps into the essence of each season, turning potential mood dips into uplifting opportunities. By weaving exercise into your seasonal routine, you equip yourself with a powerful, adaptable tool to navigate the emotional ebb and flow inherent in our natural cycles.

Finding the Right Activity for Each Season is essential for maintaining your mental health throughout the year. Seasons change, bringing distinct weather patterns and daylight variations that can affect our mood and overall well-being. Having a toolkit of suitable activities for different times of the year lets you harness the power of each season, turning potential challenges into opportunities for growth.

Spring's arrival often feels like a breath of fresh air after the doldrums of winter. It's tempting to dive headfirst into all the energy and blossoming around you. Yet, this sudden surge can sometimes leave us feeling more drained than rejuvenated. To combat this, consider activities that balance renewal with rest. Gardening, for example, connects you with the earth's cycles while providing moderate physical activity. Morning yoga sessions outside can also help you mesh with the awakening world, blending invigorating stretches with the serenity of nature.

As spring tips into summer, the long, sun-drenched days offer ample opportunity for outdoor engagement. However, the extended daylight can make you feel sluggish if you don't pace yourself. Swimming is an excellent summer activity, striking a balance between physical exertion and relaxation. Whether it's wild swimming in a lake or doing laps in a pool, the water's cool embrace can refresh your mind and body. Additionally, evening walks as the sun sets can provide tranquillity, helping you transition smoothly from the day's hustle to relaxation.

When autumn rolls around, you're met with a blend of harvest abundance and creeping melancholy. This is the time to focus on activities that ground you. Apple picking and visiting farmers' markets remind you of nature's bounty and the cycle of life. Social gatherings around a bonfire can also be comforting, blending the warmth of human connection with the elemental fire. Creative activities like drawing or journaling can help you process the seasonal shift inwardly.

Winter demands a whole other set of tools in your mental health toolkit. The cold and dark can clamp down on your spirit, making it crucial to engage in activities that bring light to your days. Light therapy is scientifically backed to offset the lack of natural sunlight, but coupling it with an activity like morning reads in a light-drenched room can hold even greater benefits. Social support is also crucial in winter. Consider joining a book club or a winter sports group to maintain that human connection.

It's not just about indoor activities, though. Winter offers its unique invitations. Ice skating and skiing can get your endorphins pumping while providing the exhilaration of movement. Just remember to balance these physical activities with warmth and relaxation, like a cup of hot cocoa by the fireplace, to avoid burnout.

Moving through these activities, it's vital to stay attuned to your personal rhythm. Not everyone will gravitate to the same kind of engagement. For some, autumn might be a burst of creative energy perfect for starting new hobbies. For others, summer is a lull requiring more laid-back activities like pottery or crafting. Knowing your tendencies helps you pick the right activity for each season.

Adjusting diet and exercise along with your activity choices can enhance the benefits further. In spring, eating lighter meals rich in fresh produce can amplify the season's renewal spirit. In summer, hydrating and focusing on cooling foods like cucumbers or watermelons helps keep you in sync with the heat. Autumn invites you to embrace root vegetables and hearty soups that ground you, while winter demands warmth from your diet through spices and nutrient-dense foods like nuts and seeds.

Exercise customisation follows a similar rhythm. Spring's energy can be harnessed through brisk walks and morning runs, while summer's heat might call for gentler, water-based activities. Autumn is excellent for longer hikes, taking in the foliage, and winter might find you best served by indoor cardio routines or group fitness classes to stay motivated.

Your mental health practices also benefit from seasonal adjustment. Meditative practices like Tai Chi can be a grounding force in autumn, while winter might see you gravitating towards more introspective forms of mindfulness. Spring's burst can be channelled into dynamic practices like breathwork, whereas summer's vibrancy might best be enjoyed through outdoor meditation or simple nature immersions.

Balancing your activities through the seasons is not just about physical and mental health but also about social connections. Create a seasonal social calendar to keep in touch with friends and family, whether it's through spring picnics, summer BBQs, autumn potlucks, or winter holiday gatherings. These planned interactions can be the social glue that keeps you thriving all year round.

Finally, don't overlook the synergy between individual and communal activities. Solo pursuits like reading or gardening can find a wonderful counterpoint in group activities, which often provide the communal support necessary for well-being. Seasonal volunteering can combine both, offering the personal satisfaction of helping others with the community engagement that sustains mental health.

Think of your seasonal activity choices as a dynamic process, continually evolving as you tune into your needs and the natural world around you. As you cultivate this adaptive approach, you'll find each season bringing its unique gifts and opportunities for enhanced well-being. By carefully selecting the right activities, you're not only managing the seasons but learning to flow with them, creating a harmonious life rhythm that thrives year-round.

Establishing this seasonal toolkit allows for a lifelong adaptation strategy, letting you mitigate mood dips and energy fluctuations that might otherwise go unmanaged. Consider keeping a journal to note what activities work best for you in each season, allowing you to refine your approach year after year.

The path to balanced mental health through seasonal changes requires intention, flexibility, and a bit of trial and error. By committing to finding the right activities for each season, you empower yourself to weather any mood or energy shifts, creating a resilient and vibrant approach to life. Whether it's the emerging buds of spring, the full bloom of summer, the rich tones of autumn, or the quiet snows of winter, there's beauty and balance to be found in every season.

The Importance of Sleep

Sleep is a cornerstone of mental health, particularly when it comes to managing our mood throughout the changing seasons. A good night's sleep isn't just the body's way to defragment; it's fundamental to emotional and mental resilience. As the days get longer or shorter, our internal clocks—known as circadian rhythms—fall out of sync, leading to feelings of irritability, increased stress, and even depression. Consistent sleep patterns can mitigate these fluctuations, offering a buffer against seasonal mood swings. Embrace the power of sleep by creating a restful environment and maintaining a bedtime routine that aligns with seasonal sunlight changes. In doing so, you're equipping yourself with one of the most robust tools in your mood-management arsenal, setting a strong foundation for a more balanced and fulfilling life throughout the entire year.

Aligning Sleep with Seasonal Changes is more crucial than many of us realise. Sleep, an essential pillar of health, is deeply affected by the cyclical nature of our environment. As the seasons shift, our body's internal clock, known as the circadian rhythm, must adapt accordingly. Understanding how to align our sleep patterns with these changes can make a significant difference in our mood and overall well-being.

In spring, as the daylight hours extend, our bodies naturally gravitate towards waking up earlier. This abundance of light can lead to increased energy levels, but it might also result in what some call 'spring fatigue'. This paradox occurs because the spike in activity can sometimes outpace our body's ability to adjust, leading to feelings of exhaustion despite the invigorating environment. To mitigate this, try to gradually adjust your sleep schedule starting a few weeks before spring arrives. Aim to wake up and go to bed 15 minutes earlier each week until your sleep pattern aligns with the earlier sunrise.

Summer offers the longest days of the year, which can be both a blessing and a curse. Longer daylight hours can enhance wakefulness and energy, yet the increased exposure to light can sometimes interfere with melatonin production, the hormone responsible for sleep regulation. To ensure a restful night during summer months, incorporate blackout curtains to maintain a dark sleeping environment. Additionally, maintaining a consistent bedtime routine, perhaps including a short period of relaxation or meditation before sleep, can signal to your body that it's time to wind down, despite the lingering evening light.

As we transition into autumn, the days grow shorter, and the diminishing daylight can significantly impact our sleep. Decreased exposure to sunlight might lead to a drop in serotonin levels, contributing to feelings of sluggishness and even depression. Try to get outside during midday when the sun is at its peak, as this can help regulate your circadian rhythm and uplift your spirits. Consider using a lightbox or dawn simulator that mimics natural sunlight, helping your body maintain a proper sleep-wake cycle.

Winter, often typified by long, dark nights and short days, tends to nudge us towards longer sleep durations. While it may seem natural to hibernate, oversleeping can sometimes exacerbate feelings of lethargy and sadness. To counter this, try to keep a consistent sleep schedule, going to bed and waking up at the same times every day, regardless of the darkness outside. Incorporate light therapy into your morning routine to simulate sunrise and help cue your body that it's time to start the day.

Furthermore, temperature regulation plays a pivotal role in aligning sleep with seasonal changes. Summer heat can disrupt sleep, so maintain a cool bedroom, ideally between 15.5 to 19.4 degrees Celsius. In contrast, winter calls for a warmer sleeping environment, but still cool enough to enable the body to naturally drop its core temperature, promoting deeper sleep stages. Use breathable bedding and adjust your thermostat to suit the seasonal shifts.

Seasonal allergens also pose a threat to restful sleep. Spring, with its blooms, and autumn, with falling leaves, can wreak havoc on those with allergies. Employing air purifiers in your home and ensuring regular cleaning practices can help minimise allergen exposure. Additionally, keeping windows closed, especially during high pollen times, can create a more sleep-conducive environment.

Psychologically, the changing seasons bring about shifts in mood and stress levels that can indirectly affect sleep. The holiday season in autumn and winter, while joyous, can bring stress and disrupt sleep routines. Practising stress management techniques, such as journalling, mindful breathing, or yoga, can help maintain a balanced mind and promote restorative sleep.

It's essential to listen to your body and adjust your sleep habits if you're experiencing insomnia or waking up fatigued. Quality sleep is not just about quantity but also about consistency and creating a restful environment. Experiment with different sleep strategies across seasons to find what works best for you, ensuring that you're in sync with nature's rhythms.

Engaging in regular physical activity tailored to each season can also positively affect your sleep patterns. For instance, a morning jog in the spring sunshine can help regulate your circadian rhythm, while a calming evening walk in the crisp autumn air can promote relaxation and readiness for sleep. The key is to stay active and adapt your exercise routine to the changing daylight and weather conditions.

Moreover, diet profoundly influences sleep quality. Consuming seasonal foods rich in sleep-promoting nutrients can support your body's natural biorhythms. For example, summer's abundance of fresh fruits and vegetables provides essential vitamins and antioxidants, while autumn's root vegetables and winter's hearty soups offer comforting and nutritious fare that can enhance relaxation and sleep.

Incorporating relaxation techniques aligned with each season can also promote better sleep. Summer might be the perfect time for evening swims or practising outdoor tai chi, capturing the lingering daylight's tranquillity. In contrast, winter months are ideal for indoor relaxation methods, such as warm baths with essential oils or evening stretches by the fireplace. Tailoring your relaxation techniques to the seasons ensures your body and mind are prepared for restful sleep.

Creating a sleep sanctuary that adapts to seasonal changes is another practical strategy. Transform your bedroom in accordance with the seasons - light, airy fabrics and colours in summer, and cosy, warm textures in winter. The physical transformation of your sleeping space can psychologically prepare you for sleep and align you with the natural cycles.

Finally, do not underestimate the power of routine. Establishing a bedtime routine that incorporates rituals specific to each season can train your body to wind down and signal it's time for rest. Whether it's sipping herbal tea in winter or practising sunset yoga in summer, these practices can harmonise your internal clock with the external environment.

Aligning sleep with seasonal changes is a proactive approach to managing mood and mental health throughout the year. By understanding and respecting the natural rhythms and bodily cues that each season brings, you can foster a sleep routine that supports your overall well-being, transforming potential seasonal challenges into opportunities for restorative, rejuvenating sleep.

Cultivating Mindfulness and Relaxation

Mindfulness and relaxation are crucial allies in managing mood throughout the changing seasons. By practising mindful awareness, you can foster a mental environment that helps mitigate the ups and downs brought by nature's cycles. Start with simple meditation techniques to anchor yourself in the present moment. Breathing exercises can ease anxiety and help you stay grounded. Just a few minutes a day can make a world of difference. Invest time in activities that promote relaxation, such as yoga or gentle stretching, regardless of the season. Consider creating a dedicated relaxation space in your home, a sanctuary where you can retreat when life's seasonal challenges feel overwhelming. This journey towards mindfulness is not just about coping but flourishing and finding balance amid change. Make relaxation a priority, because a calm mind can navigate the most tumultuous seasonal shifts with resilience and grace.

Meditation and Breathing Techniques can serve as powerful allies in managing seasonal mood variations. When you're facing a dip in spirits due to shorter days or an unexpected bout of spring fatigue, practising mindfulness can offer a sense of grounding and calm. Meditation isn't just about sitting cross-legged in silence; it's a versatile tool that can be adapted to fit into your daily routine, helping you navigate the seasonal shifts with more ease and grace.

One of the simplest ways to begin is by focusing on your breathing. Breathing techniques can be profoundly effective, often acting as an immediate balm to stress or anxiety. To start, try a basic deep breathing exercise: inhale slowly through your nose for a count of four, hold for four, exhale through your mouth for four, and then pause for another four. This cycle, often referred to as "box breathing," can help reset your nervous system, bringing about a sense of calm almost immediately.

Spring often brings renewed energy, but it can also include a type of fatigue that leaves you feeling out of sync. During this time, guided meditations focused on energy balancing can be particularly beneficial. Visualisation techniques, where you imagine drawing in the fresh, vibrant energy of the season with each inhalation, can revitalize your spirits. Similarly, visualising the release of stale, wintery lethargy with each exhale can help align your body and mind with the awakening nature around you.

Summer, with its long days and increased social activities, can sometimes feel overwhelming. Here, mindfulness meditation can help you remain centred. Practising mindful awareness, where you focus on the present moment without judgment, can make a significant difference. Spend a few minutes each day sitting quietly, paying attention to your thoughts, sensations, and the sounds around you. This practice can help ground you, providing a constant amid the hustle and bustle of summer life.

As summer gives way to the quieter, introspective season of autumn, meditation can function as a bridge to inner peace. This is a good time to practice loving-kindness meditation, which involves focusing on sending positive thoughts and compassion to yourself and others. Start by silently repeating phrases like, "May I be happy, may I be healthy, may I be at peace." Gradually extend these wishes to others, from loved ones to strangers. This form of meditation can combat the isolating feelings that may arise as the days grow shorter and cooler.

Winter, often associated with the "blues," can challenge your emotional equilibrium. Incorporating meditation into your daily life can help you navigate these darker months. Body scan meditations, where you methodically focus on different parts of your body, can be especially soothing. Lying down or sitting comfortably, bring your attention to your toes and work your way up to the top of your head, noticing any tension or discomfort. This practice not only promotes relaxation but also enhances body awareness, which can be invaluable in a season where physical activity might be limited.

To enhance your meditation practice, consider integrating it with breathing exercises tailored for specific outcomes. For instance, if you're looking to lift your mood, try the 4-7-8 breathing technique: inhale for a count of four, hold the breath for seven, and exhale slowly for a count of eight. This can enhance the relaxing effects of your meditation, making it easier to manage stress and elevate your mood, regardless of the season.

Email meditators will benefit from setting aside a dedicated time and space for their practice. Early mornings are excellent for setting a calm tone for the day, while evenings can be ideal for winding down. Find a quiet, comfortable spot where you won't be disturbed. A regular meditation session, even if it's just five to ten minutes, can create a sanctuary of calm amidst seasonal changes.

Group meditation sessions can also be incredibly supportive. This is where community often comes into play. Whether it's a local meditation group or an online session, meditating with others can foster a sense of connectedness. This shared experience of seeking peace and balance can be especially comforting during tougher seasons, like the depths of winter or the unpredictability of autumn.

Additionally, integrating a mindful breathing ritual into your outdoor activities can be transformative. Whether you're taking a leisurely walk in the park or gardening in your backyard, practice mindful breathing. Pay attention to the rhythm of your breath, the feel of the earth beneath your feet, and the breeze on your skin. These moments of connectedness with nature can significantly enhance your mood and mental clarity.

Remember, meditation and breathing techniques aren't one-size-fits-all. What works for one person might not resonate with another. It's crucial to explore different methods and find what feels most natural and effective for you. Experiment with various practices, noticing how your body and mind respond to each.

Also, consider combining your meditation practice with other forms of relaxation, such as listening to calming music, using essential oils, or practising gentle yoga poses. These can augment the calming effects of meditation and provide a holistic approach to managing seasonal mood variations.

As you cultivate a meditation practice throughout the year, you'll likely notice a cumulative effect. The strategies you employ to navigate the energy bursts of spring might evolve into deeper, quieter practices in winter. And that's the beauty of meditation—it adapts with you, offering different tools for different times.

Ultimately, the goal is to create a toolbox of techniques that you can draw upon as needed. Whether it's a quick breathing exercise to reset your day or a longer meditation session to explore your inner landscape, these practices will equip you to handle seasonal fluctuations with greater resilience and joy.

By embracing meditation and breathing techniques, you're not just reacting to seasonal changes but proactively enhancing your well-being. Consider each breath and each moment of mindfulness as an investment in your mental and emotional health. With persistent practice, you'll find yourself better equipped to transform the challenges of each season into unique opportunities for personal growth and equilibrium.

Chapter 7:
Engaging with Nature and Community

The shifting seasons offer a unique chance to tune into both the natural world and the people around you. Engaging with nature, whether through leisurely walks, gardening, or simply soaking up some sunlight, can drastically elevate your mood and invigorate your senses. It encourages a profound relationship with the environment that does wonders for mental clarity and emotional balance. On the flip side, building and maintaining a supportive community acts as a social anchor, providing vital emotional support. Participating in group activities like community events, sports, or even volunteering can create a sense of belonging and shared purpose. These communal interactions not only brighten your day but also fortify your resilience against seasonal mood dips. Integrating nature and community engagement into your routine, therefore, isn't just a mere suggestion but a powerful strategy to enhance your well-being year-round.

Reconnecting with the Outdoors

In the whirlwind of busy lives and digital distractions, it's easy to forget the simple yet profound benefits of stepping outside. Reconnecting with the outdoors isn't just a whimsical suggestion; it's a powerful antidote to the seasonal mood fluctuations many of us experience. Immersing yourself in nature can significantly bolster your mental health, giving you a break from the overstimulation of modern life. Whether it's a leisurely walk through a local park, a weekend hiking expedition, or tending to a small garden, these activities offer both physical and emotional benefits. The fresh air, the vibrant colours, and the sounds of nature work synergistically to lift our spirits and ground our thoughts, fostering a sense of peace and well-being. With every step taken beneath the open sky, we reconnect not only with the world around us but also with ourselves, promoting resilience and a deeper appreciation for the natural rhythms of life. By making a conscious effort to integrate outdoor activities into your routine, you can transform the challenge of seasonal mood changes into a journey of growth and connection.

Nature Walks and Gardening are two timeless activities that can prove indispensable for managing seasonal mood variations and enhancing mental well-being throughout the year. They collectively ground us, offering solace amidst the frenetic pace of modern life. Besides, they're profoundly accessible avenues for engaging with nature, requiring little more than time and a willingness to immerse oneself in the natural world.

Let's start with *nature walks*. Walking outdoors, whether in a park, a forest, or along a beach, inherently connects us to the cycles and rhythms of nature. It's an intuitive act, reminding our bodies and minds of our evolutionary origins. When you walk, you're engaging a host of senses – the crunch of leaves underfoot, the scent of damp earth, the sight of swaying trees, the touch of a cool breeze on your skin, and the sound of birds chattering. This sensory immersion can be incredibly grounding, helping to dissolve the stress and anxiety that can build up, particularly in the more challenging seasons.

Studies show that regular walking in a natural environment can alleviate symptoms of depression and anxiety. This is especially pertinent in cooler, darker months when we might feel more inclined to stay indoors. Walking outside, even in brisk temperatures, exposes you to natural light, which can be a natural antidote to the winter blues. The simple act of moving forward, putting one foot in front of the other, can symbolise progress and momentum, countering feelings of stagnation.

Meanwhile, **gardening** offers another dimension of engagement with nature - one that is active and tactile. When you garden, you're literally working with the earth. This physical interaction with soil, plants, and the intricate ecosystem of a garden can have profound psychological benefits. There's a reason horticultural therapy is a recognised and effective intervention for mental health.

Gardening is cyclical, echoing the seasonal cycles. Planting a seed in spring, nurturing it through summer, harvesting in autumn, and preparing the soil in winter can create a rhythm that aligns with the natural world. This can help individuals find stability through the predictability of these cycles, fostering a sense of purpose and connection.

One of the underappreciated aspects of gardening is its capacity to teach patience and mindfulness. Plants don't grow overnight; they require care, attention, and time. This process can encourage mindfulness, as you focus on the moment and the task at hand. The repetitive actions of digging, planting, watering, and weeding are meditative, providing a quiet space to reflect and unwind.

Incorporating community elements, both nature walks and gardening can become social activities. Joining a local walking group or a community garden project can provide opportunities to connect with others who share similar interests. This not only mitigates feelings of isolation, which can exacerbate seasonal mood disorders but also builds a support network that fosters communal well-being.

For those who might feel daunted by the idea of gardening, starting small can be incredibly effective. Even a few potted plants on a balcony or windowsill can make a difference. Observing the growth of a single plant you've nurtured can be deeply satisfying and serve as a microcosm of the larger cycles of nature.

The seasons offer various opportunities to engage in nature walks and gardening unique to each time of year. In spring, the world reawakens, providing a vibrant backdrop for walks filled with the scent of blossoming flowers and the sight of new growth. Spring gardening can be especially invigorating, as you plant the seeds and anticipate the blooms and harvests to come.

Summer walks, under the lush canopy of trees or along the sun-drenched beaches, can rejuvenate and invigorate. Long days encourage extended time outdoors, enhancing your exposure to the vitalising effects of sunlight. Gardening in summer is about tending to growth, managing weeds, and reaping the early rewards of your efforts with fresh produce and vibrant flowers.

Autumn walks offer a different kind of beauty, with the world painted in shades of orange, red, and yellow. This season can be incredibly introspective, with the falling leaves serving as a poignant reminder of the cyclical nature of life. Gardening in autumn focuses on harvesting the fruits of your labour and preparing the garden for the coming winter months – a fulfilling endeavour that creates a sense of achievement and closure.

In winter, while it might seem less appealing to walk outside, the brisk, cold air can be remarkably refreshing. Embrace walks wrapped in warm clothing; the stark beauty of a snowy landscape or the serene quiet of a frost-covered morning walk can be surprisingly uplifting. Winter gardening involves more planning and preparation, ensuring that your garden is ready for the next cycle of growth. This planning can be cathartic, giving a sense of purpose and anticipation for the coming spring.

Research suggests that spending at least 120 minutes a week in nature can significantly boost well-being. Whether it's through regular short walks or a weekly garden session, finding time to incorporate these activities into your routine can be a game-changer for your mental health.

As you engage in these activities, remember that there's no 'right' way to walk or garden. It's about finding what works for you and enjoying the process. Some might prefer solitary walks to mull over thoughts, while others might find joy in walking with a friend or a pet. Similarly, some might take delight in growing flowers, while others might prefer the practicality of growing their vegetables.

Ultimately, nature walks and gardening offer more than just physical activity; they provide a pathway to mental clarity, emotional balance, and a profound connection to the natural world. They are practices that, once incorporated into your routine, can provide a bedrock of stability and joy, no matter the season.

Building a Supportive Community

In times when the seasonal effects start to chip away at our mental well-being, the comfort of a supportive community can be a lifeline. Surrounding ourselves with people who understand or are willing to empathize with our seasonal challenges creates a nurturing environment where we can thrive. Whether it's through joining a local group, participating in community events, or simply fostering closer relationships with neighbours and friends, building these connections is vital. It's about creating a network where people uplift one another, exchange tips, and possibly even share in some of the practical strategies discussed in this book, such as mindfulness and outdoor activities. The sense of belonging and mutual support helps us to counteract seasonal mood dips, giving us a stronger foothold to tackle life's ebbs and flows. So, start by reaching out and weaving those threads of connection; often, you'll find others are just as eager to build the community you need.

Engaging in Social Activities is more than just a pleasant pastime; it's a crucial component of maintaining mental well-being throughout the seasonal shifts. When our social calendar thins out during colder months or becomes overwhelming in the summer, our mood can take a hit. Understanding the importance of social activities and making a concerted effort to engage in them year-round is a powerful strategy to navigate the emotional ebbs and flows associated with each season.

Humans are fundamentally social creatures. Our ancestors relied on social bonds for survival, gathering around fires, sharing food, and working together to meet challenges. In modern times, while the way we connect has evolved, the need for social interaction remains. Disconnectedness can amplify feelings of depression and anxiety, particularly when it's exacerbated by seasonal changes. To counteract this, the deliberate integration of social activities into your routine can make a significant difference.

Think of the seasonal changes as a call to adapt your social habits. During spring, when the world wakes up from its winter slumber, it's an excellent time to reconnect with friends and family you might have seen less of during the colder months. Plan a get-together, perhaps a picnic in a local park, to share in the uplift created by longer days and blooming flowers. This seasonal renewal is not just about nature; it's also an opportunity to renew social connections.

In contrast, summer can be a trickier time to maintain balance. The bright, long days often lead to a frantic social calendar. Barbecues, beach trips, and festivals can clutter your schedule, leaving little downtime. While it's tempting to say "yes" to every invitation, it's important to find a rhythm that allows for social interaction without leading to burnout. A well-curated social calendar, balancing lively outings with serene evenings, can help maintain mental equilibrium.

As autumn arrives, bringing cooler, shorter days, there's often a natural inclination to turn inward. This season, often seen as a prelude to the introspective nature of winter, is a perfect time to foster deeper connections. Engage in activities that promote meaningful interactions, like book clubs or intimate dinners with close friends. The communal aspect of harvest festivals and holidays like Thanksgiving can also be rich opportunities to strengthen bonds.

Winter can present the most significant challenge to staying socially active, partly because the cold and early darkness naturally encourage hibernation-like behaviour. Yet, this is precisely when maintaining social connections becomes critical. Seasonal Affective Disorder (SAD) and winter blues can be mitigated with the warmth of social interaction. Organising regular get-togethers, game nights, or even joining a club can provide crucial social boost during these colder months.

It's essential to understand that the quality of social interactions often trumps the quantity. A few meaningful connections can provide more emotional support than a broad but shallow social circle. Take the time to nurture relationships, ensuring they remain sources of joy and support rather than stress.

During any season, volunteering is a powerful way to engage socially while also fulfilling a deep-seated human need to help others. Volunteering can provide a sense of purpose and belonging, which are incredibly beneficial to mental health. Whether it's helping at a community kitchen during the harsh winter months or participating in neighbourhood clean-ups in spring, these activities can create a sense of community and connection.

Let's not forget that technology, while often seen as a culprit in social isolation, can also be a powerful ally. Virtual meetups, online gaming with friends, or even regular Zoom catch-ups with family members can bridge the gap when physical meetings are impractical. This is especially pertinent during the colder months or for those who live far from loved ones.

Creating traditions, no matter how small, can add structure and something to look forward to in the social landscape of our lives. Annual events like a summer beach trip with friends, winter holiday gatherings, or even a monthly movie night can provide islands of stability and joy in the ever-shifting seas of seasonal change.

Furthermore, actively seeking out new social connections can be enriching. Classes, meet-up groups, hobby clubs, or even local sports teams offer fresh social avenues to explore. The act of meeting new people and forming new bonds can infuse your life with renewed energy and purpose, mitigating the effects of seasonal mood variations.

It's also important to practise a bit of social self-care. Recognise when you need solitude to recharge, and learn to say "no" without guilt. Balancing social activity with personal downtime is essential for mental well-being, especially when managing the ups and downs of seasonal changes.

Lastly, let's consider the power of pairing social activities with physical ones. Whether it's a walk in the park with friends or a group yoga session, combining social interaction with physical exercise amplifies the benefits for mental health. Moving your body in the company of others creates a synergy that bolsters mood and enhances overall well-being.

In conclusion, **Engaging in Social Activities** throughout the year is not merely about staying busy; it's about maintaining a network of support that can cushion the impact of life's inevitable seasonal transitions. By actively nurturing social connections, thoughtfully balancing your social calendar, and finding joy in community activities, you can transform potential seasonal challenges into opportunities for growth and emotional health.

Volunteering and Helping Others isn't just about giving your time; it's a reciprocal exchange that benefits both the volunteer and those being helped. As the seasons change, your mood can swing along with them, and volunteering can offer a steadying influence. When you lend a hand, you aren't just aiding someone in need. You're also fostering a sense of purpose and community, which is powerful in combating seasonal mood variations.

Think about the warmth that spreads through you when you make someone smile. It's not just an emotional reaction; it's a biochemical one. Acts of kindness trigger the release of endorphins, the body's natural painkillers, creating a "helper's high." When winter's gloom sets in, volunteering can release these beneficial chemicals, helping to counteract seasonal affective disorder (SAD) and winter blues.

In spring, as the world reawakens, there's a surge of energy and inspiration. However, this can also be accompanied by spring fatigue, a kind of malaise as our bodies adjust. Volunteering during this period can channel renewed energy into productive and fulfilling activities. Instead of feeling aimless or overwhelmed, you can redirect this vitality into meaningful engagements, providing structured opportunities to harness your enthusiasm.

Summer isn't always as carefree as it appears. Social expectations might multiply, and not everyone thrives under the extended daylight. Volunteering offers a way to stay engaged without the pressure of constant socialisation. The routine and sense of purpose can be incredibly grounding when the long days start to feel never-ending or too chaotic.

When autumn arrives, and the leaves start to fall, so can our moods. There's a historic sense of preparation during harvest time. Volunteering can replicate this rhythm of collecting and giving, storing up good deeds and community bonds that will sustain you through the colder months. Additionally, focusing on others can distract from the often introspective and melancholy tone that autumn can bring.

Winter brings its own set of challenges, with reduced daylight often leading to a dip in serotonin levels. Social isolation can become more pronounced. Volunteering not only brings light into someone else's life but also keeps you connected. Whether it's helping at a food bank or mentoring someone, these activities can mitigate feelings of loneliness and sadness by keeping you active and involved.

Beyond combatting seasonal mood variations, volunteering cultivates a continual sense of belonging. When you consistently offer your time, you're building a network of support. This network is often reciprocated, with those you've helped becoming a source of encouragement and aid for you. The bonds forged through shared efforts can be particularly resilient, seeing you through various personal seasons, regardless of the calendar.

Another significant advantage of volunteering is the structure it introduces into your life. Seasonal changes can disrupt your routine, leading to feelings of instability. Regular volunteer commitments provide a sense of predictability and control. You know you'll be needed, and this anticipation can bolster your mood and outlook.

Moreover, when you volunteer, you develop new skills and capabilities. This not only enhances your self-esteem but also your mental agility, keeping your mind sharp and focused. Learning and practising new tasks or roles drives personal growth, an often rewarding counterbalance to the physical or emotional lethargy that seasonal changes can impose.

Part of managing seasonal mood variations is broadening your focus away from self-concern. Volunteering shifts your perspective outward, providing a break from rumination and self-involvement. This broader view can illuminate your own challenges in the context of a larger community, offering relief from the anxiety and stress that can escalate when you're constantly inward-looking.

Additionally, interacting with diverse groups exposes you to different perspectives and life experiences. These encounters can offer new insights and coping strategies you might not have considered. They remind you that you're not alone in your struggles and that others, too, navigate the ebb and flow of seasonal changes.

Consider engaging in environment-based volunteering. Activities like community gardening, tree planting, or local clean-up events ground you in the natural cycle of the seasons. They reinforce a connection to the earth, helping you align your internal rhythms with external changes, fostering a sense of harmony and balance.

Volunteering also keeps you physically active. Whether it's delivering meals to the elderly or participating in fundraising runs, these activities boost your overall health. Physical exercise is a crucial component in mood management, improving not only your physical condition but also lifting your spirits and combating feelings of inertia or stagnation.

Remember that there's no one-size-fits-all approach. Find a cause that resonates with you, whether it's animal welfare, education, health services, or crisis intervention. When aligned with your values and interests, volunteering brings not only external rewards but deeply personal fulfilment, transforming the act into a source of ongoing joy and satisfaction.

In conclusion, **Volunteering and Helping Others** plays a significant role in mood management throughout the seasons. By offering your time and skills, you create a web of support and purpose that can help you navigate the yearly cycle with resilience and grace. Harness this opportunity not just for those you assist, but for your own mental and emotional well-being. In helping others, you truly help yourself.

Chapter 8:
Special Considerations

While the general shifts in mood and energy throughout the seasons can often be managed with lifestyle adjustments, there are instances that require more focused attention. Some individuals may experience mood fluctuations that persistently interfere with daily life, warranting professional intervention to restore balance and function. Children, too, are susceptible to these seasonal changes, and recognising the signs early can offer them essential support during critical developmental stages. Furthermore, the workplace isn't immune to the ebb and flow of seasonal moods. Creating a supportive environment can significantly improve productivity and employee satisfaction year-round. Addressing these special considerations with a nuanced approach ensures that no stone is left unturned, allowing everyone to thrive despite the changing seasons. By understanding the unique challenges faced by different age groups and settings, we can provide tailored strategies that foster resilience, joy, and contentment year-round.

Dealing with Persistent Seasonal Mood Disorders

Addressing persistent seasonal mood disorders often requires a multifaceted approach that acknowledges the cyclical and sometimes stubborn nature of these conditions. While occasional mood changes with the seasons are normal, when these feelings persist, it signals the need for a deeper intervention strategy. Understanding your own symptoms and triggers is crucial. This often involves a fusion of lifestyle adjustments, such as maintaining a balanced diet and regular exercise routine, with more targeted treatments like light therapy or cognitive behavioural therapy (CBT). Routine check-ins with mental health professionals can make a significant difference, as they can help customise strategies tailored to your needs. Integrating supportive practices such as mindfulness, social connection, and community engagement can amplify these benefits, turning seasonal struggles into opportunities for personal growth and enhanced well-being. Remember, persistence and patience are key; transformation takes time, but it's within reach.

When to Seek Professional Help can be a challenging question to answer, especially when the symptoms of seasonal mood changes overlap with those of other mental health conditions. It's essential to recognise that it's entirely okay and often critical to seek professional assistance when managing your mental health through the changing seasons. Knowing when to reach out isn't always straightforward, though. Let's delve into some scenarios and signs that might indicate it's time to consult a professional.

First and foremost, if your mood changes are significantly disrupting your daily life, it's time to get help. You might find that your energy levels are so low that you can't manage your usual activities, or perhaps you're experiencing such intense anxiety that it's difficult to function. There are times when the line between 'normal' seasonal adjustment and a more serious issue can become blurred. When your symptoms begin to affect your work, relationships, or overall enjoyment of life, professional intervention can provide the support you need.

Another key indicator is the persistence and severity of your symptoms. It's normal for everyone to feel a bit down or tired as the seasons change. But, if these feelings are pervasive and long-lasting, extending beyond a couple of weeks, they might point to something more serious than just 'winter blues' or 'spring lethargy'. This is especially true if your moods are making it difficult to get out of bed, maintain personal hygiene, or keep up with responsibilities at home and work.

While self-help strategies and lifestyle adjustments can be incredibly beneficial, they're not always enough. Sometimes, even the most robust personal strategies can't fully address your mental health needs. For example, suppose you've tried improving your diet, changing your exercise routine, and cultivating mindfulness, but still find yourself struggling. In that case, a mental health professional can offer tailored interventions.

Additionally, the presence of suicidal thoughts or self-harm is a clear and urgent sign that you need professional help immediately. No amount of at-home remedies or social support can replace the critical, potentially life-saving care that professionals can provide in these situations. If you're ever contemplating self-harm, contact emergency services or go to the nearest hospital as soon as possible.

Physical symptoms that accompany mood changes should also not be ignored. For some, seasonal mood changes can manifest with physical ailments such as headaches, stomach issues, or inexplicable aches and pains. If you notice a pattern to these symptoms coinciding with mood depressions, consulting a healthcare provider can help rule out other potential causes and address the root of your discomfort.

It's also essential to consider professional help if you're finding it increasingly difficult to regulate your emotions or if your reactions are more intense than usual. Perhaps you're more irritable, prone to sudden outbursts, or tearful over things that wouldn't normally affect you. These could be signs of deeper emotional or psychological issues that a therapist or counsellor could help untangle.

For those with a history of mental health issues such as anxiety, depression, bipolar disorder, or any other chronic condition, proactive engagement with a mental health professional as the seasons change can be beneficial. Adjustments to treatment plans, whether they involve medication or therapy, can better prepare you for seasonal transitions and mitigate some of the distress these changes might otherwise bring.

Professional help isn't just about medication or intensive therapy sessions. Sometimes, what you need is guidance on effective coping strategies or new behavioural techniques to manage stress and mood fluctuations better. Cognitive-behavioural therapy (CBT), for instance, is highly effective for many people dealing with seasonal mood disorders. A professional can personalise these approaches for your specific situation.

Another valuable aspect of professional help is the accountability it provides. Regular check-ins with a mental health professional ensure that you're consistently working towards better mental health and not letting self-care strategies fall by the wayside. This ongoing support can make a significant difference, especially through the more challenging seasons.

Let's also not forget the stigma often associated with seeking mental health care. It's crucial to view seeking help as a strength rather than a weakness. Overcoming internal and external stigma can be a massive hurdle, but doing so opens up a path to genuine, sustainable well-being. Cultural shifts are happening, and your decision to seek help can also contribute to breaking down these harmful misconceptions.

Support can also come from group therapy or support groups. Meeting others who experience similar challenges can provide unique insights and foster a sense of community and belonging. These groups are often facilitated by professionals who guide the discussions and ensure that they remain beneficial and supportive.

In couples or family therapy, professionals can help you and your loved ones understand and navigate the impacts of seasonal mood changes. Sometimes our mood fluctuations affect not just us, but also those around us. Professional guidance can help create a more supportive home environment and improve relationship dynamics.

Lastly, never underestimate the importance of early intervention. The sooner you address your struggles with professional help, the better your chances of navigating the complexities of seasonal mood variations successfully. Waiting until your symptoms are severe can make the situation more difficult to manage.

Seeking professional help is a powerful step towards maintaining your well-being throughout the year. By recognising the signs early and taking action, you're empowering yourself to harness the changing seasons for personal growth and better mental health.

Children and Seasonal Mood Variations

Children are often more sensitive to the changing seasons than we might imagine, displaying mood variations that can sometimes be as pronounced as those seen in adults. It's essential to be attentive to how these shifts affect young minds, particularly since children might not have the vocabulary to express their inner experiences. Pay careful attention to changes in their behaviour, sleep patterns, and energy levels as the seasons change. Simple strategies such as maintaining a consistent routine, encouraging outdoor play, and ensuring they get ample sunlight can make a significant difference. By supporting our children through these seasonal transitions, we can help them develop resilience and a better understanding of how nature's cycles influence their emotions. Empowering children with the tools to recognise and manage their seasonal mood variations sets the stage for healthier lifelong habits and a deeper connection with their own emotional well-being.

Recognising Signs and Offering Support is paramount when it comes to children experiencing seasonal mood variations. Children, just like adults, are susceptible to the changing seasons, which can have a notable impact on their mental health and overall well-being. Identifying the signs early and providing necessary support can significantly improve their quality of life.

Children may not always have the vocabulary to express their feelings effectively. Hence, it's essential to be observant and notice any deviations from their usual behaviour. Signs of seasonal mood changes can include increased irritability, withdrawal from social activities, changes in sleeping patterns, and fluctuations in appetite. Recognising these subtle cues can be the first step in addressing the problem head-on.

One of the key indicators could be a noticeable dip in their school performance or sudden reluctance to attend school. Children who are generally enthusiastic about their studies might become disinterested or distracted. Teachers can play an essential role in recognising these signs and collaborating with parents to provide a consistent support system both at school and home.

Once you've identified potential signs, it's crucial to approach the child with empathy and patience. An open conversation where they feel safe to express their feelings can be very enlightening. Avoid direct questioning that might feel like an interrogation. Instead, gentle prompts like "I've noticed you seem a bit different lately. Want to talk about it?" can often yield more honest responses.

Offering support might sometimes mean making minor adjustments to their daily routine. Extra sleep or adjusted extra-curricular activities can make a difference. Encourage regular physical activity tailored to the season—whether it's a summer swim or a winter walk—to help release endorphins and reduce the impact of seasonal mood changes.

A balanced diet rich in nutrients can also play a significant role in mood regulation. Foods that boost mood, such as those rich in omega-3 fatty acids, can be integrated into their meals to naturally uplift their spirits. Ensure that these dietary changes are enjoyable for the child; no one wants to be forced into eating food they dislike.

Another method to alleviate seasonal mood impacts is light therapy. Particularly in the darker months, exposure to natural light or light therapy boxes can make a substantial difference. Consider setting up a bright, cosy corner with ample natural light where your child can play, read, or even do their homework.

Emotional and psychological support can also be extended through mindfulness exercises and relaxation techniques. Introducing your child to age-appropriate mindfulness practices, such as guided imagery or simple breathing exercises, can offer them tools to manage their emotions more effectively.

Encouraging social interaction is vital. Whether it's playdates, group activities, or family outings, ensuring that the child remains socially engaged can ward off feelings of isolation. It often helps to plan these activities according to the child's interest to keep them motivated and excited.

As much as you, as a parent or caregiver, might want to be the primary source of comfort for your child, don't hesitate to seek additional help. Professional support, such as child psychologists or counsellors, can offer specialised techniques and therapies tailored to your child's needs.

Informing and involving school staff in your child's struggles can provide them with a better understanding and enable them to offer additional support during school hours. They might be able to make accommodations, such as providing additional breaks or a quiet space for your child when needed.

Beyond individual support, fostering a supportive community atmosphere can create a more holistic approach to managing seasonal mood changes in children. Engaging in community activities or support groups can facilitate shared experiences and strategies among parents and children alike.

Don't underestimate the power of creative expression. Encourage your child to take up hobbies like drawing, painting, or writing as an outlet for their emotions. Creativity can act as a powerful medium for children to articulate feelings they may struggle to express verbally.

Being proactive in these areas not only helps in managing the seasonal mood changes effectively but also equips your child with strategies they can use lifelong. The knowledge that someone is there for them, attentively caring and ready to support, can bolster their confidence and resilience.

The Workplace and Seasonal Moods

Undoubtedly, the ebb and flow of seasons can have a profound impact on our professional lives. In the workplace, fluctuating moods due to seasonal changes can influence everything from our concentration levels to our interpersonal relationships. Creating a supportive work environment is crucial for mitigating the adverse effects of seasonal mood variations. Simple adjustments, like incorporating more natural light, adjusting workloads to better align with energy levels, and promoting regular breaks, can make a massive difference. Proactive measures like team activities that enhance well-being, mental health resources, and open communication channels about mood-related challenges are essential for fostering a resilient and understanding workplace. By acknowledging and addressing these seasonal impacts, employers and employees alike can transform potential mood slumps into opportunities for enhanced productivity and well-being, paving the way for a more harmonious and motivated team throughout the year.

Creating a Supportive Work Environment is essential for maintaining well-being throughout the year. Our workplaces play a significant role in our lives, often influencing our mood and mental health more than we realise. As the seasons change, so do our needs and the challenges we face, making it crucial to foster a work environment that supports everyone's mental and emotional health.

The first step in creating a supportive work environment is addressing the physical workspace. Lighting is a key factor—natural light can significantly impact mood and productivity. During the darker months, consider full-spectrum lighting or light therapy lamps that mimic natural daylight. Not only does this help combat the winter blues, but it also keeps energy levels stable.

Temperature control is another important aspect. Have the necessary resources to maintain a comfortable temperature in the office, whether that means providing fans during the summer or extra heating options in the winter. Personal comfort directly affects concentration and work efficiency.

An inclusive and flexible work culture can greatly ease the seasonal pressures on employees. Encourage flexible working hours or remote work when appropriate. This flexibility allows individuals to manage their time better, fitting in exercise, daylight exposure, and other activities that help counteract seasonal mood variations.

It's also vital to nurture a social environment where colleagues feel comfortable discussing their well-being. An open-door policy can be instrumental in this regard. Employees should know they can approach management with concerns about their mental health without fear of judgement or repercussions. This openness fosters a sense of security and support within the team.

Peer support programs and mental health initiatives can further strengthen the workplace. Regular workshops or seminars on mental health awareness can educate staff on recognising symptoms and applying coping strategies. Additionally, having trained mental health champions within the workplace can provide immediate support and guidance to those in need.

Break times should be considered sacred, offering a chance to decompress and recharge. Encourage taking breaks away from desks to reduce screen time and promote physical movement. Creating dedicated break areas with comfortable seating and a relaxing atmosphere can make a world of difference. Simple changes like introducing plants, soothing colours, and art can significantly enhance these spaces' aesthetic and mood-boosting qualities.

Regular team-building activities can also alleviate seasonal stress. Organise outdoor events during pleasant weather or indoor gatherings that include light physical activity, creative workshops, or mindfulness sessions. These activities not only break the monotony but also strengthen team cohesion and morale.

Furthermore, consider the availability of nutritious snacks and drinks in the workplace. Offering healthy options can help stabilise mood and energy levels. Look into seasonal superfoods that boost mood and immune function, providing both immediate and long-term benefits to employees' overall well-being.

Workload management is another crucial aspect. Recognise that productivity levels can fluctuate with the seasons and plan accordingly. Adjust project timelines and expectations to accommodate these natural variations. Overloading employees during their lower energy phases can lead to burnout and decreased overall productivity.

Provide access to professional mental health services either on-site or through an employee assistance program (EAP). These services can offer confidential support and resources for those struggling with significant stress or seasonal affective disorder (SAD).

Encourage regular feedback from your team about the workplace environment and their well-being. This ongoing dialogue can highlight areas for improvement and ensure that changes made are effective and appreciated. When employees see that their input is valued and acted upon, it boosts morale and fosters a culture of mutual respect and ongoing improvement.

Start small if necessary. Even minor adjustments, like revising dress codes to accommodate seasonal weather, can show employees that their comfort and well-being are priorities. Celebrate achievements and milestones openly, offering recognition not just for work-related successes but also for personal progress and well-being initiatives.

Lastly, remember that a supportive work environment is a dynamic entity. What works in summer may not be ideal for winter, necessitating regular reviews and adjustments. Stay flexible and willing to try new approaches, always keeping the ultimate goal in mind: to create an environment conducive to the well-being and growth of everyone involved.

Incorporating these strategies can transform the work environment into a sanctuary that not only sustains productivity but also actively enhances the well-being of its inhabitants throughout the seasons. When we feel supported at work, we're in a better position to meet both our professional and personal goals, regardless of what the weather outside is doing.

Conclusion

As the seasons change, so too do the rhythms of our lives. We've explored the highs and lows that come with each passage of nature's cycle, delving into the energy bursts of spring, the languid days of summer, the reflective nature of autumn, and the quiet of winter. Our aim throughout has been to equip you with the tools and insights needed to manage these seasonal shifts and, importantly, harness their potential for mental and emotional well-being.

Understanding the unique challenges and opportunities presented by each season gives you a framework to anticipate and respond effectively. The world around us is in constant flux, and so are we. Recognising the signs of Seasonal Affective Disorder (SAD) or more minor seasonal mood fluctuations is the first step in taking control of your mental health throughout the year. By doing so, we turn potential stumbling blocks into stepping stones for deeper personal growth.

Spring often comes with a wave of renewed energy, but it can also bring unexpected fatigue. As we've discussed, balancing this paradox involves embracing natural rhythms and paying attention to diet and exercise. By nourishing your body with the right foods and activities, you lay the foundation for enduring vitality. Spring is a time for planting seeds, both literally and metaphorically, setting intentions for the year to come.

The vibrancy of summer can be invigorating, yet extended daylight can sometimes lead to a feeling of lethargy. Creating a daily routine that includes staying cool and engaging in outdoor activities can help you maintain motivation. Mindfulness practices are incredibly beneficial during this time, fostering a connection with the present moment and enriching your experience of the season.

With autumn's arrival comes a duality: the bounty of the harvest coupled with the onset of darker days. For some, this marks the beginning of seasonal depression. Understanding the trigger factors and creating a comforting environment can make a significant difference. Autumn encourages us to gather and prepare, not just in a physical sense but emotionally, building a network of connections to sustain us through the colder months.

Winter, though often seen as bleak, offers a unique opportunity for reflection and restoration. Combatting the winter blues may require practical solutions like light therapy or seeking warmth, both physically and socially. Engaging in seasonal activities and maintaining a support network help mitigate feelings of isolation, turning what might seem like a dormant period into one of meaningful stillness and regeneration.

Throughout the entire year, certain constants remain: the importance of a balanced diet, regular exercise, adequate sleep, and mindfulness practices. These are the cornerstones of mood management, regardless of the season. Tailoring these practices to fit the seasonal context enhances their effectiveness, making it easier to navigate life's ebbs and flows.

Engaging with nature and community fosters a sense of belonging and purpose. Whether it's through nature walks, gardening, or social activities, these connections are invaluable. Volunteering and helping others can provide a boost to mood and offer perspective, reminding us that we are part of something larger than ourselves.

Special considerations like persistent mood disorders, accommodations for children, and the influence of seasonal moods in the workplace underscore the need for a holistic approach. Professional help should not be overlooked when necessary. Establishing a supportive work environment and recognising the signs of seasonal changes in children ensures a proactive stance, benefiting overall well-being.

The essence of this book is empowerment. By aligning with the seasons rather than resisting them, we can transform our relationship with life's natural rhythms. Each season carries its own wisdom, and by tuning into this, we become more attuned to ourselves and our needs.

This journey through the year, with its uphills and downhills, reminds us of the cyclical nature of life itself. There's a time for growth, a time for flourishing, a time for harvesting, and a time for rest. Embracing these phases allows for a fuller, richer experience, both emotionally and mentally.

As you continue moving forward, keep these insights and strategies at the forefront of your mind. Reflect on how the seasons have impacted you in the past and think about how you can adapt the practices learned here to enhance your future well-being. Consider this book not a final destination but a guide for ongoing personal transformation.

Remember, resilience lies in adaptability. By observing, understanding, and responding to the changing seasons, you cultivate a more resilient and adaptable mindset. This flexibility supports emotional balance and long-term mental health, giving you the tools to face any seasonal challenges with confidence and grace.

Ultimately, your journey is unique. While the natural world follows a universal rhythm, each person's experience within it is wonderfully distinct. Trust your instincts, honour your needs, and approach each season with curiosity and openness.

In conclusion, may the knowledge and strategies shared here empower you to live harmoniously with the seasons. Harness the opportunities they bring, and turn potential challenges into moments of growth and self-discovery. Let each season be a chapter that enriches the story of your life.

Thank you for embarking on this journey of understanding and managing the seasonal effects on your mood and mental health. May you find peace, joy, and well-being in every season of your life.

Appendix A:
Appendix

The journey through the changing seasons offers an array of experiences, emotions, and challenges. As we've navigated the intricacies of seasonal moods and their impact on mental health, it's essential to have resources that can further empower and support your endeavours. This appendix serves as a valuable companion, providing additional tools and insights to help you harness the benefits of each season while mitigating its challenges.

Resources for Further Reading and Support

Diving deeper into the subject can be immensely beneficial. Whether you're seeking academic research, practical guides, or personal stories, there is a wealth of information available. Here are a few curated options:

Books: Consider exploring books by experts in the field of seasonal mood variations and mental health. These can offer in-depth knowledge and practical advice.

Articles and Journals: Academic journals and articles provide the latest research findings and can give you a well-rounded understanding of the subject.

Online Platforms: Websites, blogs, and forums dedicated to mental health and seasonal changes can be a source of community support and updated information.

Professional Organisations: Reaching out to mental health organisations can provide access to support groups, counselling services, and educational materials.

Seasonal Recipes for Mood Enhancement

The food you consume plays a significant role in your mental well-being. Incorporating seasonal, mood-boosting recipes into your diet can be a delightful way to maintain balance. Here are a few ideas:

Spring: Fresh salads with leafy greens, colourful vegetables, and a light vinaigrette can invigorate your senses.

Summer: Try chilled soups or smoothies packed with berries, cucumbers, and mint to keep cool and refreshed.

Autumn: Warm, hearty stews with root vegetables and grains can provide comfort and nourishment.

Winter: Indulge in soups and casseroles rich in proteins and healthy fats for warmth and sustenance.

Sample Exercise Plans for Each Season

Physical activity is another cornerstone of mental health management. Tailoring your exercise routine to align with the seasons can enhance your energy levels and overall mood. Here are some suggestions:

Spring: Engage in outdoor activities like hiking or cycling to take advantage of the mild weather and blooming landscapes.

Summer: Swimming or early morning runs can help you stay active while avoiding the peak heat of the day.

Autumn: Consider brisk walks through scenic parks or joining a local sports league.

Winter: Indoor activities such as yoga, pilates, or even a home workout routine can keep you active despite the cold.

This appendix is designed to be a springboard for further exploration and action. While seasonal changes can often bring challenges, equipped with the right strategies and resources, each season can also be an opportunity to enhance your well-being and growth. Continue to explore, adapt, and thrive throughout the year.

Resources for Further Reading and Support

As you delve into the complexities of managing your mood and mental health through the changing seasons, it's crucial to have access to additional resources and support. With a wealth of information available, curating a list of reliable and insightful resources can make a world of difference on your journey to maintaining well-being throughout the year. Here are some valuable resources that can provide further reading and support.

Books and Literature

There are numerous books that explore the subject of seasonal mood variations and offer practical advice. For a deep dive into Seasonal Affective Disorder (SAD), consider reading "Winter Blues" by Norman E. Rosenthal. This seminal work offers a comprehensive look at SAD, offering both scientific insights and practical solutions. For a broader understanding of the mind-body connection, "How to Be Human" by Ruby Wax provides a blend of humour and neuroscience, making mental health an accessible topic.

Scientific Journals and Articles

For those inclined towards academic research, scientific journals such as the "Journal of Affective Disorders" provide peer-reviewed articles on the latest studies related to mood disorders and their seasonal impact. Accessing databases like PubMed can also help you stay up-to-date with the most recent findings in this field. These resources can offer a deeper understanding of the mechanisms behind seasonal mood changes and emerging treatments.

Online Communities and Forums

Connecting with others who share similar experiences can be incredibly empowering. Online forums, such as those found on platforms like Reddit or HealthUnlocked, host vibrant communities where members discuss their experiences with seasonal mood variations and share tips for coping. Being part of such a community can provide emotional support and practical advice.

Professional Organisations

Several professional organisations offer resources and support for those dealing with seasonal mood changes. The Seasonal Affective Disorder Association (SADA) in the UK, for instance, provides information, research updates, and helplines. Similarly, the American Psychological Association (APA) offers resources on seasonal mood disorders and can guide you in finding a qualified therapist.

Apps and Technology

Technology has become a valuable tool in managing mental health. Apps like "Happify" and "MoodKit" offer activities and tools designed to improve mood and mental well-being. Light therapy devices, such as lightboxes, can also be particularly beneficial in combating the winter blues. Brands like Lumie offer a range of products specifically designed to mimic natural sunlight and help regulate your circadian rhythm.

Support Groups and Therapy

Face-to-face support groups can provide a sense of community and understanding. Organisations such as Mind in the UK and the National Alliance on Mental Illness (NAMI) in the U.S. offer local support groups and counselling services. Cognitive Behavioural

Therapy (CBT) has also proven effective for managing seasonal mood changes, so seeking out a CBT therapist could be a worthwhile step.

Educational Workshops and Webinars

Attending workshops and webinars can deepen your understanding and provide practical strategies. Many mental health organisations offer seasonal workshops focusing on coping mechanisms and lifestyle changes. Check out the offerings from institutions like The Mental Health Foundation or The Centre for Mindfulness for engaging and informative sessions.

Blogs and Websites

Blogs and websites dedicated to mental health can offer a more personal perspective. Websites like *Psyche* and *Psychology Today* feature articles written by experts, as well as personal stories from those affected by seasonal mood variations. These platforms can provide relatable content and practical advice.

Natural and Holistic Approaches

If you're interested in natural and holistic methods, several books and websites focus on these approaches. For example, "The Nature Fix" by Florence Williams explores the restorative power of nature and its positive impact on mental health. Websites like *Wellness Mama* offer tips on using diet, exercise, and mindfulness to manage mood throughout the seasons.

Mental Health Organisations

National and international mental health organisations offer a wealth of resources. The World Health Organisation (WHO) provides global insights and guidelines on mental health, while local organisations such as Rethink Mental Illness in the UK offer region-specific resources and support services. Their websites often feature helplines, informational guides, and directories for finding local support.

Emergency Support

In times of crisis, knowing where to turn is crucial. Emergency helplines such as the Samaritans in the UK or the Suicide & Crisis Lifeline in the U.S. provide 24/7 support for those in immediate need. It's important to have these numbers readily available should you or someone you know require urgent assistance.

Mindfulness and Relaxation

Practicing mindfulness and relaxation techniques can be incredibly beneficial. Apps like "Headspace" and "Calm" offer guided meditations and relaxation exercises tailored to different seasons. Journals and gratitude journals can also serve as valuable tools for reflecting on your journey and maintaining a positive outlook.

Diet and Nutrition Resources

Maintaining a balanced diet can significantly impact mood and mental health. Websites like *BBC Good Food* and books such as "The Good Mood Food" offer recipes and meal plans designed to enhance mood and energy levels. Nutritionists and dieticians can also provide personalised advice tailored to your specific needs.

Exercise and Fitness Services

Engaging in regular physical activity is pivotal for managing mood. Fitness platforms like *Yoga with Adriene* on YouTube or fitness apps such as "Nike Training Club" offer guided workouts and routines tailored to all fitness levels. Local gyms and fitness centres often provide classes that can help you stay motivated and active throughout the seasons.

By utilising these resources, you'll be well-equipped to navigate the seasonal fluctuations in mood and mental health. Remember, the journey to well-being is ongoing, and having the right tools and support can make all the difference. As you continue to explore and incorporate these resources into your life, you'll find yourself better prepared to embrace the challenges and opportunities that each season brings.

Seasonal Recipes for Mood Enhancement

When discussing the ebb and flow of our moods throughout the year, it's important not to overlook the power of what we consume. Food isn't just fuel; it's a tool that can help manage our mental well-being. From the bright greens of spring to the hearty roots of winter, our diet can be tailored to complement the season and stabilise our mood.

Spring often feels like a breath of fresh air after the cold, dark winter months. The longer, sunnier days can lift our spirits, but they can also bring about spring fatigue. Incorporating fresh, vibrant ingredients into our meals can help mitigate this. Think of leafy greens, asparagus, and radishes. A simple spring salad with these ingredients, drizzled with a light vinaigrette, provides a burst of energy and nutrients. Dishes like this are not just about nutrition; they're about revitalising the senses, stirring excitement for the season.

Summer's warmth and extended daylight hours often bring a sense of freedom and happiness. However, the heat can also be draining, and the temptation to reach for sugary drinks and snacks is strong. Instead, try hydrating, cooling foods like watermelon, cucumbers, and mint. A refreshing watermelon salad with feta and mint is a great way to stay cool while keeping your mood balanced. It's satisfying yet light, and it helps maintain hydration.

Grilling in the summer is another fantastic way to enhance your mood. The act of cooking outdoors contributes to a sense of well-being, and the social aspect of barbecues provides connection. Grilled fish or chicken paired with a side of quinoa and grilled vegetables makes for a balanced meal that fuels your body and uplifts your spirit.

Autumn, with its rich colours and cooler temperatures, often brings about a sense of melancholy as the days shorten. But it's also a season of harvest, a time to enjoy the abundance of hearty vegetables and fruits. Root vegetables like sweet potatoes, carrots, and beets are perfect for roasting. A warm bowl of roasted vegetable soup can be comforting and grounding. The natural sweetness and earthy flavours provide not just nourishment, but a sense of contentment and stability.

To counteract the autumn blues, consider incorporating apples and cinnamon into your diet. Baked apples with a sprinkle of cinnamon and a dollop of Greek yoghurt can be a delightful dessert. The aroma of cinnamon is known to reduce irritability and fatigue, making it a great addition during this season.

Winter, often synonymous with cold and darkness, can be the most challenging season for maintaining a positive mood. Comfort foods become essential, but comfort doesn't have to mean unhealthy. Think of hearty stews packed with vegetables, legumes, and lean meats. A lentil stew with carrots, potatoes, and spinach not only warms the body but also nourishes the mind. The slow, steady energy release from such meals helps keep your mood stable throughout the day.

Spices like ginger, turmeric, and cloves can be particularly beneficial in winter. Not only do they add depth and warmth to your meals, but they also have anti-inflammatory properties and can boost your immune system. A cup of turmeric ginger tea in the evening can be both soothing and health-enhancing.

Don't underestimate the power of citrus fruits in winter. Oranges, grapefruits, and lemons are rich in Vitamin C and can help ward off winter colds. A citrus salad with mixed greens, avocado, and a citrus vinaigrette can be a vibrant, mood-lifting meal on a grey winter day.

Throughout all seasons, the importance of staying hydrated cannot be overstated. Water aids in almost every bodily function, including brain function, which is directly tied to your mood. Herbal teas, flavoured with fresh herbs or a slice of lemon, can be a pleasant way to increase fluid intake.

Being mindful about what you eat and tuning into seasonal cues can transform your approach to diet. Rather than seeing food as a mere necessity, view it as an ally in your journey to mental wellness. This connection between what you consume and how you feel is a powerful tool for mental health management. It's about creating a holistic balance, where every bite you take can be a step towards better mental well-being.

Remember, preparing and sharing meals can also be a source of joy and connection. Invite friends over for a seasonal cooking session or make it a family activity. The act of cooking itself can be meditative, providing a sense of accomplishment and focus.

In summary, tailoring your diet to align with the seasons can offer a natural, effective way to manage your mood throughout the year. By integrating fresh, seasonal ingredients into your meals, you harness the inherent benefits they bring. This way, you don't just eat to live; you eat to thrive.

It's not just about finding recipes that fit the season but about creating a lifestyle that honours the natural rhythms of the earth. By doing so, you cultivate a deeper connection with your food, your body, and the seasons, enhancing your overall well-being.

Seasonal recipes are more than just a diet; they're a practice, a tradition, and a celebration of the unique offerings of each time of year. Embrace them, and you'll find that the journey through the seasons becomes a bit brighter, a bit more vibrant, and a whole lot more nourishing.

So, dive into the seasonal bounty, explore new ingredients, and let nature's changing palette inspire your culinary creativity and uplift your spirit.

Sample Exercise Plans for Each Season

Adapting our exercise routines according to the seasons can make a significant difference in our overall well-being. Each season brings unique environmental conditions that can either motivate or demotivate us to stay active. Tailoring your exercise plan to fit the seasonal vibes not only makes it more enjoyable but also manageable. Let's explore how you can keep moving through all four seasons with simple yet effective exercise plans.

Spring: Embrace the Renewal

Spring, often seen as a time of renewal, is perfect for integrating fresh activities into your routine. The warming weather and blooming nature inspire us to get outside and move. Consider starting with:

Walking and Hiking: Enjoy nature trails and parks, observing the budding trees and flowers. Aim for a brisk 30-minute walk or a weekend hike.

Cycling: Dust off your bike and take it for short rides around your neighbourhood or local parks. It's a great way to increase cardio-vascular fitness while enjoying the scenery.

Yoga in the Park: Outdoor yoga sessions can help you stretch and strengthen your body while soaking up the springtime sun. Look for local yoga groups or start your own routine with online videos.

As the weather transitions, pay attention to your body. Start slowly and gradually increase your activity level to avoid injury and spring fatigue. Remember, this season is about awakening both mind and body.

Summer: Harness the Brightness

Summer's long, sunny days can supercharge your motivation, making it an ideal time to ramp up your exercise routine. However, it's also crucial to stay cool and hydrated. Here are some summer-friendly activities:

Swimming: An excellent full-body workout, swimming keeps you cool while benefiting your cardiovascular system. Whether in a pool, lake, or ocean, this activity is both refreshing and healthy.

Morning Runs: With extended daylight, opt for early morning runs to beat the heat and start your day with an endorphin boost. Even a 20-minute jog can do wonders.

Group Sports: Engage in social sports like beach volleyball, tennis, or football. These sports not only enhance physical fitness but also foster social connections, essential for mental well-being.

To avoid summer fatigue or dehydration, make it a habit to exercise during cooler parts of the day, either early mornings or late evenings. Hydrate well and incorporate light, breathable clothing. This will help you maintain a sustained and enjoyable routine.

Autumn: Balance Harvest and Reflection

Autumn, with its crisp air and changing colours, brings a sense of both harvest and preparation. It's the perfect time to reflect and adjust your exercise regimen. Consider these activities:

Trail Running or Walking: Enjoy the vibrant autumn leaves by running or walking on forest trails. The uneven terrain can also improve your balance and coordination.

Strength Training: As the weather cools, indoor strength training becomes more appealing. Incorporate a mix of weight lifting, resistance bands, and bodyweight exercises.

Autumn Clean-Up Activities: Turn seasonal chores like raking leaves into a workout. These activities can help you get your heart rate up while enjoying the seasonal transformation.

Autumn is a time of grounding and preparation, making it ideal for activities that build and maintain strength. Focus on mindful movement and balance; this approach will support not only your physical health but also your mental resilience as the days grow shorter.

Winter: Warmth and Consistency

Winter's cold and shorter days can challenge even the most dedicated fitness enthusiasts. Yet, it's possible to keep your body active and mind engaged. Here's how:

Indoor Workouts: From online fitness classes to home gyms, winter is perfect for indoor activities. Consider routines focusing on cardio, strength, and flexibility. Look into yoga, Pilates, or dance aerobics.

Winter Sports: If you enjoy the cold, winter sports like skiing, snowboarding, or ice skating offer great full-body workouts. Bundle up and head to the nearest rink or slope.

Walking and Snowshoeing: Don't underestimate the power of a brisk walk in the winter landscape. Snowshoeing is another excellent low-impact, high-intensity activity.

Staying active in winter requires commitment, yet it offers a unique chance to embrace the season's beauty. Dress in layers, warm-up properly, and stay consistent to keep winter blues at bay.

Transitioning Between Seasons

As one season flows into the next, so should your exercise routine. Transition periods are opportunities to adjust your activities gradually, ensuring your body and mind adapt smoothly. Here are tips for seamless transitions:

Gradual Adjustments: Don't overhaul your routine overnight. Gradually introduce new activities, giving your body time to adjust.

Listen to Your Body: Pay close attention to how you feel—both physically and mentally—during transitions. Modify your intensity and duration based on your energy levels.

Stay Flexible: Be willing to adapt your plan. Weather changes, daylight variations, and even personal schedules can impact your routine. Flexibility ensures you stay active regardless of circumstances.

Transitioning in sync with the seasons encourages a harmonious blend of activity and rest, honouring your natural rhythms and promoting sustained well-being all year round.

Sustaining Motivation and Joy

While it's essential to maintain physical activity throughout the seasons, it's equally crucial to find joy in the process. Here are some strategies to keep your motivation high:

Set Seasonal Goals: Establish achievable goals for each season, keeping you focused and inspired. For example, aim to run a 5k in the spring or finish a strength training program by winter.

Mix It Up: Variety is key. Rotate between different types of workouts to prevent boredom and target various muscle groups.

Join a Group or Class: Sometimes, collective energy can be powerful motivation. Join seasonal sports clubs, group fitness classes, or community exercise challenges.

By finding activities you genuinely enjoy, exercise becomes less of a chore and more of a rewarding habit. Embracing the seasons with tailored exercise plans ensures you're not only physically fit but also mentally resilient, turning potential challenges into opportunities for growth and well-being.

Each season has its unique rhythm and flow, shaping how we approach our physical wellness. By aligning our exercise routines with the natural cycles of the year, we create a balanced and dynamic approach to staying healthy. Let's move through each season with intention, adapting our activities to harness the full potential of nature's changing energies.

www.ingramcontent.com/pod-product-compliance
Lightning Source LLC
Chambersburg PA
CBHW051447280526
45785CB00003B/1459